speed decorating

speed decorating

A PRO STAGER'S
TIPS AND
TRADE SECRETS
FOR A FABULOUS
HOME IN A
WEEK OR LESS

JILL VEGAS

PHOTOGRAPHS BY MICHAEL GRIMM

The Taunton Press

The Taunton Press, Inc.
63 South Main Street, PO Box 5506
Newtown, CT 06470-5506
e-mail: tp@taunton.com

Editors: Erica Sanders-Foege, Laura Wallis
Copy Editor: Anne Jones
Indexer: Lynne Lipkind
Jacket/Cover design: Jean-Marc Troadec
Interior design: Chika Azuma with Teresa Fernandes
Layout: Teresa Fernandes
Photographer: Michael Grimm

Library of Congress Cataloging-in-Publication Data
Vegas, Jill.
  Speed decorating : a pro stager's tips and trade secrets for a fabulous home in a week or less / Jill Vegas ;
photographer, Michael Grimm.
      p. cm.
  Includes index.
  ISBN 978-1-60085-033-2
  1. Interior decoration. I. Title.
NK2110.V39 2009
747--dc22
                                        2009020598
Printed in the United States of America
10 9 8 7 6 5 4 3 2

DEDICATION

With love and gratitude to the memory of my mom, Adriana, who always inspired me to go for it. She was the original speed decorator. Her loving and feisty spirit lives on.

To my dad, Roger, who raised an enthusiastic daughter.

To the love of my life, Michael Zimberg.

And to everyone who wants a beautiful home.

ACKNOWLEDGMENTS

Thank you to all the people who helped create *Speed Decorating* with enthusiasm and dedication: Fred Bernstein, Karen Boltax, Robert Brawley, Lisa Marie Collins, Alan Cresto, Jennifer diPretoro, Benjamin Dyett, Donna Emma, Richard Esposito, Gary Feely, Mimi and Steve Houston, Kemper Johnson, Tanya Jones, John Kantakis, Grace Kempton, Julie Maren, Erin and Sean Mclean at Shelter Island Gardens, Peter Meister, Barry Miller, Courtenay O'Sullivan, Olivia Pebbles, Jason Penney, Molly Przetycki, Julie Rice, Karen Robert, Gianluigi Romagnolo, Rosemarie Ryan, Paul Sadowski, Ori Schwartz, Lauren Stern, Garrit Van Kempen, Jenny West-D'Alba, Greg D'Alba and Spud, Jack Wettling, Susan Whitney, and Chris Woods.

To all my clients and friends for their inspiration and encouragement. To Laura Wallis for bringing this project to life; Erica Sanders-Foege at Taunton Press for editorial expertise; Jennifer Griffin at the Miller Agency for helping to get this out there; Michael Grimm for beautiful photos; my family for supporting me with unconditional love: Carolyn and Roger Nelson; Linda and Morty Jaffe. And to Michael Zimberg for his love, support, and goofy sense of humor.

Contents

122

58

17

59

23

108

155

54

IMPRESSIONIST PAINTERS

Vincent van Gogh paintings   Kröller-Müller Museum

Lucie-Smith   Visual Arts in the Twentieth Century   Abrams

INTRODUCTION

Discovering Your Inner Decorator...Now

Have you ever wished you could simply close your eyes and then open them again to find a glamorous room decorated in your favorite style? Or go on vacation for a week and return to a fabulously revived and sparkling house? Well, join the club! As wonderful as it would be to have a personal decorating fairy godmother, most of us know that it takes hard work to accomplish changes like these. The question is, how hard? How long must it take? That's where this book comes in.

When time is of the essence, *Speed Decorating* can help you turn your home into a place you truly love. Allow me to be your fairy godmother. I'll point my magic wand at every room in your house and show you, step by step, how to transform the space.

Over the years, I have worked with homeowners whose primary goal was to turn their house or apartment into a place that is really special—fast. Many were preparing to sell and wanted to create an environment that would inspire potential buyers and leave them clamoring to make the best offer.

I've developed techniques that are speedy and satisfying, and that work. With my method of speed decorating, you can turn your home into a warm, inviting place. It's the perfect solution if you're selling your house and want to make the best impression possible when your realtor arrives next weekend. It's also terrific if your dinner guests are arriving in a few hours and your kitchen desperately needs sprucing up, or if out-of-town visitors are due in a couple of days and you want to greet them with a lavish guest room.

All you need to do is dive in.

What does great style look like to you? For me, it's vibrant color; well-made, modern furnishings; and accessories in all the right places—as in this bedroom, with its wall of bold, black-and-white fabrics. Whatever look you love, you can make it happen . . . now.

3

DEFINING SPEED DECORATING

Many people are intimidated by working with a decorator and are afraid to make choices of their own. I'm here to demystify the process so that you can create a gorgeous house with confidence and ease.

I know it can be done. I've seen it happen again and again. Recently, I worked with a client, Valerie, who completely transformed her approach to decorating. A newlywed, she was overwhelmed with the challenge of decorating her first home. She had tons of questions. What color palette? What fabrics? What window treatments? How should the furniture be arranged? Without answers, she felt paralyzed.

When faced with a large room to decorate, it's easy to feel overwhelmed. Where to begin? I'll help you make priorities and create space that's as warm and inviting as this chic living room.

Working together, we started with the front door and discussed how she wanted to feel when she first walked in. We identified what she wanted to see and how she wanted the space to function. From there I showed her how furniture could support those functions and be stylish and welcoming.

That's the speed decorating method: step by step, room by room. All she really needed to do was stay focused and take one thing at a time. Once she let go of her fears, Valerie's first order of business was to buy a new dining room table and chairs because she loved to entertain. This is the way for anyone to begin. Just pick one thing and go for it!

In getting the knack of speed decorating, it's helpful to think about what this technique is *not*. It isn't traditional interior decorating. This isn't about going out and hiring a decorator to reinvent your space or setting rigid guidelines about how the process has to happen. It is not about throwing out every stick of furniture and starting over or hiring a contractor and electrician for a gut renovation and new wiring plan. This is about discovering your own "Inner Speed Decorator." When you do this, you can evaluate your own rooms, determine priorities, and get to work updating and transforming them.

Likewise, while standard decorating involves ordering custom furniture, floor coverings, light fixtures, and so on, these require weeks, even months, of waiting for delivery. The result might be the home of your dreams but the process is long and grueling.

Adding some well-placed accessories is both fast and easy—and it can go a long way toward making your space look beautiful. Here, a pair of tall vases and some flowering dogwood branches add a personal touch to a stone hearth.

Swapping out a boring light fixture for something new—like this spectacular blown glass pendant—is a job for an electrician. Calling in the help you need to get things done right will save time in the end.

Speed decorating is a refreshing alternative. It's about empowering yourself to evaluate your spaces and find immediate solutions; shopping "off the rack" and getting creative with furnishings and fixtures you already own; and doing most of the hands-on work yourself.

CALLING IN HELP

Getting your hands a bit dirty while making over your home is tremendously satisfying. It's also the fastest way to get things done. That said, there are times that even the speed decorator needs to call in outside support.

It's best to recruit an electrician to swap out light fixtures or a plumber to replace a faucet. These are small, short-term projects, and you may not be able to find someone to take them on right away. But don't let this sidetrack your work. Keep going. Tackle the things you can get done.

That was the advice I offered my clients, Judy and Paul, when helping them revamp their bathroom. We had decided to install a new faucet to go on the pedestal sink. As it turned out, they had purchased a gorgeous faucet years prior but had never gotten around to installing it. It was time to take action.

Although we had no plumber immediately available to do the installation, we kept going with the plan. We painted the room and purchased all new accessories. In the meantime, Judy polled her neighbors for references and found a wonderful plumber who would accept the task. Ultimately, the job was done on time.

The point is to keep going. Don't let the obstacle of finding a professional stand in your way.

If you're planning to replace light fixtures or install dimmers on all your switches, you'll need an electrician. Make a list of all the electrical work you need done throughout your house, and then have him come and do it all at once.

Whether decorating for company or potential buyers, remember that details count. Here, a trio of open shelves displays a distinctive collection of decorative plates and classic French soup tureens.

A kitchen must have a solid foundation to function. Ample workspace near the sink and stove, as shown in this updated country kitchen, is a key foundation element.

Likewise, a good repair person can be essential if you have water-stained walls that need patching or a new countertop to install. Ask friends and neighbors for recommendations.

This is not the time for the big construction or hard-wiring tasks (popping holes in the wall, running wires to switches, plastering, and so forth). It is about choosing the most expedient tasks, and getting help with them if you need it.

Speed decorating involves trading existing fixtures and furnishings for new ones, experimenting with arrangement and color, and filling your rooms with versatile, moveable pieces that will accentuate the assets and downplay flaws.

This is not the approach for fussy perfectionists who daydream about finding their next home and how it will be better. This is about loving the home you live in right *now*, flaws and all.

SEVEN PRINCIPLES OF DECORATING (and Why They Matter for the Speed Decorator)

These are the building blocks of every decorating project. Even a tiny task, like freshening up a powder room, will benefit from keeping these principles in mind. In fact, for the speed decorator, it is even more vital to stay focused on these details, as they'll help you formulate a plan of action.

In the chapters that follow, we'll touch on all these principles in each of the major living spaces of your house.

Calm

How do you feel when you walk into your living space? Take a deep breath. Look around. Is the space soothing, or do you get a sense of chaos and stress? If the latter, then you're probably neglecting the basics.

Before starting any decorating project, clear away clutter so you can really assess your space and make effective changes. Get rid of items that don't belong. That means removing the broken lamp that hasn't worked for years, for instance.

If you do nothing else, make sure that every room is clean and in good working order, as in this sweet country kitchen, where there's plenty of space for snack-time goodies.

Maybe you've been meaning to rewire it, but still it sits, clogging the living room corner with negative energy.

Look around and see what can go immediately. This includes looking in bookcases, underneath furniture, and on the floors. As I told my client, Pamela, cramming your space with stuff creates tension. An incredibly creative person, Pamela had an amazing design sense and owned many beautiful things. Unfortunately, all these things crowded the floors, shelves, and every available surface. What we needed to do was edit.

We kept out only a few favorite things—some sculpture, art, side tables, and lamps. We tucked the rest away in the basement and organized into categories so she could easily rotate items with the season or her mood. Pamela loved it and her husband was thrilled. He said he felt like he could finally breathe in the room. And it's true; the room did feel lighter—like a breath of fresh air!

Get Organized. Some people are natural organizers. If you're one of them—great! You can skip this step and move on. But if you're overwhelmed by clutter, help is available. You can take steps to overcome the barriers that keep you from getting and staying organized. And you can call in the pros. There are a number of professional services available, staffed by natural neatniks who will tackle the messes you don't have the time or the desire to deal with. And they'll do it fast. Some steps to consider:

- **Kick out your inner procrastinator.**
  Procrastination is the biggest enemy of speed
  decorating, so get over it! And start doing. If you're
  feeling tired or frustrated, take action. You'll be
  surprised at how quickly your mood changes. My friend
  Lisa Zaslow of Gotham Organizers recommends setting
  up a system that fits your personality, style, budget,
  and habits. If you create a system for paying bills and
  filing at your desk, for keeping clothes in order in the
  closet, and so on, everything will be streamlined.

- **Hire a professional organizer.** For a fee, an organizer
  will create those systems for you, and make sure they
  work for your lifestyle. They can revamp your rooms,
  your cabinets, your closets, and clear them of unnecessary
  stuff, and then help you keep them clutter-free. Look
  online at the National Association of Professional
  Organizers (napo.net). They have a searchable database,
  so you can easily find a pro near you.

- **Call a junk removal service.** Knowing what has to go is only half the battle.
  Finishing the job means getting rid of the stuff! If you don't have time for yard
  sales, trips to the local dump, and so on, hire a service to come and haul away
  everything in one shot. Check the phonebook for services in your area, or look
  at 1800GOTJUNK.com. For a reasonable fee, they will come and remove your
  excess stuff, recycling or donating whenever possible.

Condition

This goes hand-in-hand with creating a sense of calm in your home. Once you've
moved aside the stuff that camouflages the bones of your rooms, it's time to do a

---

●●○ FIVE SPEED CLEANING TIPS

1. **Clear the clutter first.** Remove piles of papers,
   mail, and magazines. Put it all in a basket to
   read or recycle later. Make one pass through
   each room and gather anything that doesn't
   belong, such as dishes, old magazines, and
   stray socks.

2. **Wash the windows.** Sparkly clean windows
   allow natural light to pour into the room,
   creating a fresh vibrant feeling.

3. **Check walls for scuff marks.** A Mr. Clean
   Magic Eraser® will get rid of them fast.

4. **Replace any burned out bulbs,** and don't
   put the fixture together again without first
   washing the globe with warm soapy water.

5. **Brighten hardwood floors.** Don't bother with
   special products. Just damp-mop them with
   white vinegar and water, then buff with a
   clean cloth so they shimmer.

There are infinite ways to add style to your home. Choose artwork you love, find a furniture style that speaks to you, dig out a collection and display it creatively. A quirky grouping of drawings, a dramatic red painting, and a collection of glass fish are just some of the details that make this mid-century modern–inspired living room come alive.

deep clean. Scrub every corner, every baseboard, and every light switch until not a speck of dust remains. I like to work with organic and all-natural cleaners, such as white vinegar and baking soda, to do an effective job without any nasty chemicals.

While you work, make a note of any necessary repairs, and get them done as soon as possible. If you detest cleaning, hire someone. If you don't have the skills for certain repairs, find a handyperson who does. But get it done.

Style

This is the visual expression of who you are. The difference between a bland, generic living space and one that feels personal, welcoming, and vibrant.

Anyone can go to a store and buy something. But style is not something you can buy. It's all in how you put it together. Style is about mixing your favorite furniture with accessories you love to create an original room. It's about having the courage to try something new.

If you're walking along the beach and see a beautiful piece of driftwood, bring it home! Try it out as a banister or a coat rack. Try a new paint color, or several. Even

●●● SPEEDY WAYS TO FIND YOUR STYLE

- Think about what inspires you. Look at clippings from magazines (see "Speed Toolbox," on page 21 for tips on keeping this all in one place). Mark the pages in this book when you see a style you like. If you've been taking digital pictures of things you love, browse through them all. Look for a pattern to emerge, such as a similar color or style.

- Look at furniture, artwork, and collectibles you already own. Hand-me-downs aside, what purchases have you made? Is there a particular look or color scheme that you keep coming back to?

- Consider the style and size of your home. It might seem obvious, but if you've recently moved, what

worked in your old living room may not be what you need for the new living room. American colonial style pieces might feel out of place in a contemporary home, for instance; likewise, that overstuffed, grand-scaled sofa might be claustrophobic in a compact, bungalow living room.

- Buy only what you love. You don't have to be matchy-matchy and buy everything from a set. Take the time to create your own look.

- Have fun! Invest in what you love. With some smart, creative accessorizing, you'll see a big difference.

A properly arranged room makes your life easier. Here, groupings of furniture define areas for conversation, and other activities, and the whole space feels open and welcoming.

For a beautifully arranged bookshelf, break up rows of books with objets d'art. Here, a collection of seashells, small paintings, and a statue, which also acts as bookend, mingle with well-loved novels.

if you look around your rooms and see lots of hand-me-downs and uninspired architecture, you can find terrific, fast fixes that will add zest to your surroundings in no time. Be creative and confident.

Arrangement

The basic principles of good arrangement are easy. Once you define the function of certain areas, it's a cinch to arrange and rearrange furniture and accessories. It's also a lot of fun and allows you to be creative and imaginative.

One of the benefits of proper arrangement is good flow. This is a sense of motion and harmony in a space. It creates a positive feeling in a room and makes for flexible spaces.

To encourage flexibility, incorporate light pieces of furniture that do double duty. An ottoman, for instance, can function as a footrest when you're sitting quietly and reading and can transform into an entertaining station when an tray of hors d'oeuvres is placed on it. And, in some instances, it can provide overflow seating when moved to the dining room table.

Make sure each room has an ease about it. You should be able to walk freely without tripping over anything. Like a winding nature path, the flow should be effortless and organic. Nothing is in your way, but you're not stuck with a stiff, geometric arrangement in which all the furniture is pressed against the walls, creating a black hole of dead space.

Light

Proper lighting gives a warm, inviting atmosphere. Your approach to lighting will depend on the room you're in: While the kitchen and bathroom demand bright, clear task light, the dining room and bedroom require a softer, romantic light.

Getting lighting right means thinking about the fixtures themselves (does their style please you? is the level of light adjustable?); the glow they cast (too soft for

A collection of interesting bottles and sea fan enhance the natural theme of this bathroom.

work? too clinical for romance?); and placement in the room (shadows aren't always bad, it's where they are that counts).

In the chapters that follow, I'll walk you through creating an amazing lighting scheme for every room—and outside, too.

Color and Texture

If you're living in a world of beige, it's time for a new era. Can you imagine a world where everything was beige? Look at nature for inspiration. There's texture, color, and breathtaking patterns just about everywhere you look. A red cabbage is one example. It has rich, vibrant jewel tones mixed with softer hues and organic lines. That shows how a gorgeous accent color complements a more muted background shade.

Or, for a study of both color and texture, think about moss along a trail. It's spongy and lush, and its colors range from powdery, silver green to emerald velvet. In a living room, that combination might translate into a silvery rug and a plush, dark green mohair sofa.

Color inspiration can come from almost anywhere. My friend Fred Bernstein, who owns the store Home 114 on New York's Shelter Island has an amazing eye for color. He uses contrasting hues in the most imaginative ways. For example, in the bathroom he redecorated, he created a refreshing, spa-like experience with vibrant shades of blue and green. It makes me feel like I'm at a luxury resort in Turks and Caicos, where the water is pure and the plants are blooming in abundance.

When thinking of color and texture, use your imagination. Look to your favorite destination or vacation spot or maybe one of your favorite moments and translate that experience into a palette.

Details

This is signature speed decorating: using art, arrangements, and accessories to give your home instant personality. They're fast and easy to change—with your mood, or the season, or the theme of a particular occasion.

You can quickly transform a sofa from summery lightness to winter coziness by swapping out pillows and throws to fit the season. When you change your closet from bathing suits to cashmere sweaters, why not take the time to give your living room a seasonal update, too.

You may want to update your family photos or frame some new pictures to change the feeling of a room. And don't forget fresh flowers! I recommend you bring in new ones for a quick lift whenever you're expecting guests. It's a small investment for a

Adding color can be the fastest way to breathe new life into a room. Here, a pair of sapphire velvet armchairs lends a conversation corner a feeling of luxury. A vase in the same hue plus pillows and a throw in jewel tones are rich finishing touches.

Use details to tell your guests a bit about yourself. One look at the items on display here reveals the homeowner to be a lover of all things nautical. This arrangement works because the theme is apparent but it doesn't—ahem!—go overboard.

Bunches of deep red flowers, arranged in a collection of fun, mis-matched vases, are a vibrant focal point in this airy room.

●●● SPEED DECORATING QUESTIONNAIRE

When evaluating any part of your house, inside or out, ask yourself these questions:

- **What are the primary functions of the space?** Does it suit them? In the kitchen, for instance, you need to be able to work freely, and you need comfortable accommodations for the friends who will gather there. The bedroom, by contrast, should primarily be conducive to quiet time, relaxation, and romance.

- **How does the room look?** Try to see your space as if visiting your home for the first time. Is the furniture shabby? Is the wall color faded? Is the whole place chaotic and cluttered?

- **Is everything working?** Check for those details we tend to ignore when we live with them every day: burnt-out bulbs, wall cracks, water damage, torn upholstery. Now is the time for repairs.

- **Does the room feel comfy and inviting?** If you're happy with your basic furniture and everything is in good repair but still something feels "off," take a look at the details. Maybe you have too many hard surfaces and need an infusion of softness and color, like some pillows, a throw, or a new rug. Or maybe the lighting isn't right. It should be bright enough for the task at hand but also be warm and flattering, not harsh.

Write down the answers to these questions. This is a quick way to pinpoint the challenges that most need addressing. During this process, snap some digital pictures of the area and analyze them. This is a great way to get a fresh, objective viewpoint from which to make an evaluation. The photos will also be handy to have when shopping later—they'll jog your memory and provide easy reference.

---

big impact. You might even buy some potted, flowering bulbs, such as paper whites; they'll last longer than cut flowers, and will make the room smell delicious for days.

Bringing the outdoors in is one of my favorite ways to transform a room. In the spring, think about cutting forsythia branches for a vivid splash of yellow. The arrangement you create doesn't have to be fussy or expensive—even cuttings of wildflowers in a glass mason jar will look great.

Keep it simple. When I was first married, I thought I needed to have fancy crystal vases as a sign that I was officially an adult. But the problem was that I kept dropping them! After the third vase shattered, I decided not to replace it. Instead, I use glass cylinder vases, silver julep cups, or whatever looks interesting in the pantry. Sometimes it's my grandma's Fiestaware pitcher; other times it's a carafe with white lilies.

THE THREE-STEP PROCESS

Whenever I work with a client, I take a three-step approach: evaluate the situation, explore solutions, and then take action. And as you read the chapters in this book, you'll see that I tackle every room the same way.

It's easy to rush into quick fixes when time is tight but resist that impulse. Slow down and take the time to assess where you are and where you want to go. It's always the best and most efficient way to work.

STEP 1: **Evaluate the Situation**

Take a good look at whatever room you're in and ask yourself if it's meeting your needs, if it makes you happy. Think about the mood you're in when you spend time in the space and about the mood you'd like it to express.

Sit down with my "Speed Decorating Questionnaire," on page 19 and put your answers on paper. While doing this, start to make a list of the changes you'd like to make, as well as any repairs or housekeeping tasks that need attention.

This is also the part of the process where defining your timeline is essential. Do you have a few hours? A full week? The projects you decide to tackle will depend on this time frame. See "The Timeline," on page 25 for more on this.

STEP 2: **Explore Solutions**

This step is all about determining priorities. Review the list you started in step one and decide what can be done now, in the time you have, to make the biggest impact. You might decide to call in a handyperson for an afternoon or recruit a handy friend to help for the day. Your tasks might include cleaning and de-cluttering, rearranging existing furniture, choosing a new color scheme, and starting a shopping list to replace items as needed.

STEP 3: **Take Action**

Begin! Once you've gotten through the first two steps, it's time to get moving. You can repurpose items you already own—revamp a lamp, for instance, or paint a dresser to give it a whole new look. This is also the time to remove items that aren't working. Give them away, sell them, or relocate them to a room where they are a better fit.

●●● SPEED TOOLBOX

Working and shopping quickly and efficiently depends on having details on hand. So here's the advice I give all my clients: Buy yourself a new notebook, dedicate it to speed decorating, and keep it with you. Have it ready when you start your evaluation, and make numerous notes. The more details you record, the better. A digital camera is also an indispensable tool.

• **Your notebook is a place for inspiration:** Use it to organize clippings from home design magazines with furnishings and color schemes that you like. If you see details that inspire you at a friend's house or even in a hotel, spa, or restaurant, record those here, too, with notes and sketches. Brainstorm ideas and write them down before you forget.

• **Record vital stats in the notebook:** The dimensions of the room, sizes of existing furniture and light fixtures, the wattages of lightbulbs, and a floor plan. If you don't have a floor plan, then make a rough sketch. Keep color swatches here, too, as a reference when shopping. For your outdoor spaces, make notes about locations of plantings, trees, and shaded areas.

• **The notebook is also the place to keep your action plan.** Draw a line down the middle of a page and write "To Do" on the left side and "To Buy" on the right side. The "To Do" column is where you'll note all the things to be fixed or changed in the room. The "To Buy" column is your room-by-room shopping list.

• **Take digital pictures of each room,** and scroll through them when you're evaluating a new chair or accessory in a store. You can also snap pictures of rooms and furnishings that inspire you as you come across them in daily life, so it's smart to keep the camera handy.

• **Keep this book with you.** It's designed in a small format so you can easily take it along. Go ahead and write on the pages, and put Post-it notes on pictures you like for a quick visual reference and inspiration when shopping.

●●● SPEED SHOPPING TIPS

Shopping on a tight schedule means shopping smart. Here's my advice on how to shop efficiently:

- **Furniture stores:** Before you go, find out how long they take to deliver so you're clear before you even walk through the door what options you should check out. If all the items in the store are custom and take weeks to deliver then don't go there. Or ask the manager about any showroom pieces they're willing to sell. Typically, in January and August, showrooms are willing to sell floor items at a discounted price to make way for the new collection.

  If you have a favorite store, find out when they'll be selling floor samples. Ask a salesperson to show you the items that are in stock and available for immediate delivery. Take time to sit or lie down on pieces to make sure they are comfortable. If you're not sure about what style you like, visit a store with a variety of options so you can see what you love.

- **Online options:** I'm a touchy-feely shopper. For upholstered items, it's best to go to the showroom and sit on things to test them out. For me, linens need to be touched to be evaluated. Likewise, items where color really matters—upholstered chairs, sofas, rugs—I always buy in store. On the other hand, coffee tables, lamps, stools, and side tables are easy to buy online. You can find unique accessories, hardware, and antique fixtures online, too. Try auction sites as well as traditional retailers. Be sure to review shipping options carefully, so you'll know when to expect delivery.

- **Home improvement and "big box" stores:** When you're looking for instant results, head to the local big box retailer to find things you can buy on the spot. Inexpensive yet stylish lamps can be found here for "quick fixes," as can a wealth of organizing supplies, such as shelving. Again, look for items that

are available off the shelf.

- **Specialty stores:** If you have a good idea of what you want and prefer to shop in person, head to a specialty store. Lighting stores, bed and bath stores, kitchen supply stores, flooring retailers, paint stores—there's a category for most everything you need. Here it's critical to bring your digital camera and notebook so you can be efficient and focused. Some clients get overwhelmed with all the choices and options. The best way to shop a specialty store is to talk to a sales associate and explain exactly what you need.

- **Garden centers:** Look for native plants. Buy plants that support the environment. The days of sterile green lawns that hog the water supply are over! Ask your local nursery for advice and recommendations. Bring photos and your speed decorating notebook with measurements and digital pics, to show the area you'd like to focus on.

Speed decorating solutions aren't just about buying new things. In a home office space, for instance, a good de-cluttering and the addition of a bright bunch of flowers might be all the facelift you need!

It's okay to start small. Remember that even the tiniest touch—like this single, delicate daisy in an espresso cup on a windowsill—can go far in expressing your style.

Now it's time for the best part: Shopping. Buying new things is a blast, and it's a task worth taking your time on (within reason). You can run out and buy new accessories for a bathroom or kitchen in an afternoon. Or online, you could purchase an entire new home sitting in your bathrobe. If you're looking for larger pieces of furniture, light fixtures, or linens, you may want to allow yourself several days for browsing, making choices, and scheduling deliveries.

Whatever space you're aiming to speed decorate, the process begins with an evaluation. In an outdoor room like this screened porch, step back and consider, Is it inviting? Is it comfortable for outdoor dining? Do you love spending time there?

THE TIMELINE

It goes without saying that speed decorating means doing things fast. To that end, I've only included projects in this book that can be done in a week or less. Some take less than an hour. Of course, you probably won't be able to redo your whole house in a week but, as you'll discover, just getting started is a big step. It might seem monumental, to make a real difference in the look of your home in such a short time, but it can be done, and done well. I think you'll be happily surprised.

As you read these pages, you'll see that I've divided most tasks into one of three categories:

- **Magic-Wand Makeover:** If you only have a few hours or possibly a day to whip a room into shape, this is the instant solution for you. Ideas here could include buying new accessories, swapping out hardware, banishing clutter, or setting a festive mood with candles.

- **Mini Boot Camp:** Dedicate a long weekend (only three days!) and you can create decorating miracles. You could paint a room, replace a faucet, update kitchen cabinets, buy new linens, or create a dazzling outdoor party scheme.

- **Ultimate Boot Camp:** In one week, you will see results. This is the program if you'd prefer to have a little more time to shop or overhaul a room. Commit to something big like complete closet organization, buying and installing new light fixtures, creating a cozy reading nook, or transforming a tired bathroom into a relaxing oasis.

So choose the room you want to tackle first, pick a deadline, and write it in your calendar. Tell a friend or your spouse what you're doing so there's some accountability. Now get going! The clock is ticking.

Vivid purple Clematis, cut from the garden and arranged in a tall glass vase, make a glamorous outdoor centerpiece.

"THE FIRST RULE OF DECORATION IS THAT YOU
CAN BREAK ALMOST ALL THE OTHER RULES."

—BILLY BALDWIN

1. A Welcoming Entry

Your entry is the space that says, "Welcome to my home." When guests and
potential buyers walk inside, they instantly form that all-important first impression. Back when I used to work in advertising, we created thirty-second commer-
cials to make a positive impression on viewers. If the commercial didn't work, they
wouldn't buy the product. The same principle applies in the entry. People may not
spend much time here, but the mood you set will make the difference between
guests who instantly feel comfortable and ones who don't.

The good news: The entry is one of the easiest spaces in the house to speed
decorate. Even large foyers are fundamentally simple, so getting yours in show-off
condition in a week or less should be a cinch. What's more, if you're just getting your
feet wet with speed decorating, this is a great first project. Once you see what an
impact a few upgrades can make, you'll be ready to tackle the rest of the house!

Many entries, particularly in today's new houses, are large in scale and rather
empty, perhaps designed more to impress than to wrap your guests in a (metaphori-
cal) hug. Or, in busy family homes, they're high-traffic areas that tend to accumulate piles of shoes, scuff marks, and dirt. In apartments, entries can be tiny—hardly
big enough to linger in at all—but their style (or lack of) still makes an impression
on anyone who enters.

Remember that a warm welcome, not an intimidating or chaotic entrance,
makes for happy party guests. And if you're selling your home, that same warmth
is what helps potential buyers imagine living in your space. Fortunately, no matter
how large or small your entry, there are things you can do quickly to make it the
welcoming place you want it to be.

Coming and going is
a practical matter,
but it can be a beauti-
ful one, too. This en-
try, equipped with a
simple white-painted
schoolhouse bench
and some fluffy throw
pillows, is clean and
inviting. A red clock
and double sconce
on the wall are both
useful and stylish.

Your main entrance should make a statement. Every detail at the door of this lovely home, including well-maintained stone steps, an elegant hanging light, and boxwood shrubs in concrete planters, complement the symmetry of the architecture.

When I think of the ideal entryway, my imagination inevitably conjures my grandma's house. Growing up, we always walked through the front door when arriving for a visit. And any time of day or night, this was a cheerful place to be. The light was bright, yet cozy. And there was a sturdy old bench next to the door. This was the perfect spot to plop down and pull off our boots before making our way into the kitchen, where delicious homemade gingersnaps were waiting on the table.

These days, whenever I enter a home, I'm impressed if the entry is bright, inviting, and well organized. Bonus points if there are accessories that make a statement about the character of the home. A statement piece could be an amazing piece of art, a mirror, a fabulous pendant light, or a splash of vibrant color.

It may seem obvious to have a well-lighted entry but frequently this is over-looked. Cheery light in the entry will make your guests feel comfortable and send a message to the neighborhood that yours is a fun, festive household.

Finally, a welcoming entry is a functional one. This is every guest's first and last stop in your home. Think about what they need. Is there a place to sit down and put on shoes? A spot to lay a purse while slipping off a coat? The best entrances take care of these details.

MAKING AN ENTRANCE

No matter what your entry looks like now, you can quickly make it the space you want it to be. Here are the decorating challenges I frequently see in the entry:

- The space is in poor condition (the door squeaks, the floor is heavily scuffed, the entry rug is dingy).

- Light is lacking (dim or burned-out bulbs make the space more depressing than welcoming).

- Disorder rules (think piles of shoes and mail, and no proper home for any of it).

- Helter-skelter sense of style (the fixtures and color scheme are chaotic), or no sense of style at all (the space has been ignored, from a decorating perspective, leaving a blah, bare foyer).

All of these can be addressed in a short amount of time. On the pages that follow, you'll find solutions that fit, whether you have a few hours or a full week. This is not about renova-tion but a speedy approach to stylish decorating. The focus is on the doable details, such as updating hardware, buffing up that floor, and replacing fixtures that completely transform a

House numbers let your visitors know they've arrived. At my friend Chris's house, the numbers reside on a charming gated trellis, as an official hello before guests start up the path.

stale vibe into a truly welcoming one. I'll make sure you're ready in time, whether your friends are coming to dinner tonight or your first open house is scheduled for next weekend.

To do that, we have to start at the beginning. Remember that three-step process I outlined in the Introduction, on page 20? Here's where we put it to work. The way to start any job, from a quick spruce up for one room to a whole-house makeover, is to sit down and evaluate the big picture. Go through the "Speed Decorating Questionnaire," on page 19 and think about your answers. What kind of entry do you have? How do you feel when you walk in?

As I alluded to previously, there are three basic types of entryways. The first is the formal entry, which may be large and rather sparsely furnished and mainly used on special occasions. This type is often in need of warmth and personality. The second is the family entry, typically a back hall or mudroom entrance. This busy area probably needs a good cleaning and an efficient system to keep it organized. And then there is the all-purpose entry. In apartments and smaller houses, this modest space serves every need and often feels more overwhelming than inviting. Here, the goal is to find a peaceful, welcoming, and personal middle ground.

I saw a classic example of a formal entry that needed a personality boost when I visited Kristin, a client who called me in to assess her foyer. When I arrived, I could see why she needed help: There was no foyer. That is, the space she had didn't feel like one. When I opened the front door, I stepped into a vacant cave. There was no place to sit and take off shoes, to put keys and mail, nothing. But there was plenty of room for these things.

The main challenge was that the space had super-high, 18-foot ceilings. Kristen didn't know what size furniture she needed. She wanted something that would look proportionate to the grand entry, not be dwarfed by it. She had company arriving in one week, so we quickly needed to find pieces that worked in the space and that would give it some much-needed style.

Artwork and a few, well chosen collectibles can create a functional entrance. Here, an abstract painting found in a dumpster, a glass bowl, and a vintage suitcase surround a slim console table, making a charming vignette.

Is your foyer inviting? Offer your guests a comfy place to sit, like this plush armchair, while taking off their shoes and they'll feel right at home.

A light fixture, like this pendant lamp inset with multi-colored, rough-cut resin crystals, makes an instant style statement.

After some discussion, we chose a favorite black-and-white photo that Kristen took on a trip to Thailand as a focal point. We had it enlarged and framed and hung it, centered, on one wall. We then ordered a mid-century modern bench online. When it was delivered a few days later, we placed it below the photo to provide a place to sit and set items down.

While we waited for these items to arrive, we had the walls painted to define the space and make it cozy. The result was a useful entry that looked beautiful the moment you stepped in the door.

By making a careful assessment, like the one I did for Kristen, you can pinpoint the problems specific to your entry. Note: If the light is poor in your entry, I recommend you put in some bright bulbs before starting to evaluate. Give yourself plenty of light to scrutinize every corner. Then you'll have no excuse for overlooking details.

Of course, you'll want to arm yourself with the necessary evaluation tools: your notebook and digital camera. Remember to use them to keep track of the changes you want to make, your progress, and any relevant statistics (ceiling height, light-bulb wattages) that will help you work.

Once you've evaluated the situation in your entry, set a deadline for getting the work done. Maybe you have one already. There's nothing like knowing that any minute dinner guests or a real estate agent will be ringing the doorbell to get you moving. But if you don't have a specific event in mind and just want quick action, set a deadline anyway and write it in your calendar. (After all, who doesn't want a house that's drop-in friendly any day of the week?)

The tasks you prioritized in the evaluation questionnaire from the Introduction dictate how you work. In the entry, a lot can be done in a day. But if your time frame allows, you can go for solutions that are more elaborate. This chapter will help you find the fixes that are doable in the time you have.

Think beyond the traditional when furnishing your entry for a truly functional and gorgeous space. Here, a built-in bookcase unit separates the foyer from the living room and offers abundant storage.

Adding a distinctive piece of furniture is a speedy way to make your entry look great. This antique secretary has storage for hiding mail and a glass cabinet at the top for curiosities.

FIRST THINGS FIRST

Throughout this book, I'll remind you that basic housekeeping has to come before big fixes. That means doing a deep clean to remove dirt and grime and making necessary repairs before damage gets worse. Even if you're in a hurry, taking care of these details is essential. Well-maintained "bones" in each room form the foundation of a beautifully decorated home.

Nowhere is this as true as it is in the entry. Remember, this room is all about first impressions, and nothing makes a better first impression than an immaculate, well-organized space.

Sometimes, when you live with rooms every day, you stop noticing basic details. Not long ago I worked with Julie and Duane, who are the busy parents of four kids. She's a stay-at-home mom, and he runs his own small business. When I met them, they were preparing to sell their house, a contemporary with gorgeous classic details. They had a week to get ready to meet the realtor, and they called me in to see what they could do to improve their entry.

We started just inside the front door. I immediately saw that the paint was peeling on the door and the molding around it, and that the door's hardware was tarnished. The bench just next to the door in the foyer had obviously soiled cushions.

When I mentioned these things to Julie, she hadn't even seen them before, in spite of rushing in and out that door countless times every day. For quick fixes, we

---

●●● FIVE MUSTS FOR A GREAT-LOOKING ENTRY

1. **Clutter-free surfaces.** Get rid of boxes, shoes, anything that doesn't belong in the space.

2. **Brilliant light.** Replace any burned-out or too-dim bulbs. Clean and polish light fixtures. Get new fixtures altogether, if needed (see "Lighting the Way," on page 36 for more details).

3. **A nice-looking floor.** Vacuum and mop the floor. Replace the doormat if it's dingy. If the floor's condition is really bad, buy some floor polish and buff out scratches, or buy some carpet tiles (such as FLOR℠ brand) and make a runner to hide them.

4. **Clean walls.** Get rid of scuff marks (a Mr. Clean Magic Eraser is great for this), or touch up the paint in spots to hide them. If the walls are in really bad shape, repaint.

5. **A fabulous front door.** If the hinges squeak, oil them. If the hardware is tarnished or worn looking, get some brass or other metal polish and shine them up. If necessary, repaint the door and update its style with new hardware, or replace the entire door.

As soon as the front door opens, light should greet your guests. This ceiling fixture, visible from the outside through the transom, sparkles cheerfully.

polished the hardware, painted the door a parchment color to set off the foyer's architectural details, and cleaned those cushions. To make a statement, Julie purchased a new table lamp for the console, transforming its look. Since they love to entertain, we also created a vignette with black-and-white photos taken at past parties. This was an easy and fun way to lend a personal touch to the space.

Take a good look at the problem areas you identified during the evaluation. Then get to work making sure every surface is clean and in good repair. Hire a cleaning service if you don't want to do the work yourself.

LIGHTING THE WAY

Abundant, sparkly light in the foyer is critical. Even if your entry is super clean, if you walk in the front door and it's gloomy, it sets a negative tone. People are naturally drawn to lighted spaces, so be generous with light here—it will make your guests feel welcome. Great light also shows off all your hard work in cleaning and fixing up your foyer, and invites potential buyers to take a closer look.

One client of mine told me she bought her apartment because she loved the light and flow—meaning the way the space and the furniture in it drew her through the home. It was hard to see why she felt this way because she had installed a dim purple bulb in a stained glass light fixture in her entryway, giving the effect of a mortuary.

●●● LIGHTING RULES TO REMEMBER

- **In an entry,** it's usually best to install bulbs that are in the 60- to 75-watt range (less, of course, if you have several bulbs in one fixture). Dimmer than that and the space might feel claustrophobic or gloomy.

- **Hang your lights at the right height.** A chandelier or pendant should be hung so the tallest person you know doesn't hit his head (about 6 ft. 6 in. from the floor) and no higher. The fixture shouldn't be crowded up against the ceiling, but hung so it looks relatively centered in the space.

- **Install a dimmer switch.** This will allow you to bring the lights down for an evening party and brighten them back up again on those rainy afternoons.

- **Make sure everything sparkles.** Never let dust build up on your light fixtures; clean them routinely so they shine their brightest. Look at the switch plate, too. If it looks grimy, clean it. If it's just a bit old and boring, you can buy a new one to complement your decor. This quick update really makes a difference.

I showed her that with just a few quick additions, like a new bulb and crystal pendant light, she could transform the place. The second the front door opened, the entry felt welcoming and bright.

When you open the door to your house, you should be bathed in light. You don't want it to look like an interrogation office, but you should be able to see, and the space should be cheerful and inviting.

If your existing light fixture is too small or dim (a tiny fixture sporting a moody, 40-watt bulb, for instance), you may want to invest in a chandelier or pendant light for a brighter, more stylish look. Lighting and home stores abound with great options.

Finally, remember that a mirror can have a delightful brightening effect, even in a small foyer. I love mirrors because they are among the speediest of speed decorating fixes. There is an abundance of styles to be found, from baroque numbers in gilded, carved frames to sleek, minimalist models—and you can easily buy one and hang it in the course of a few hours. Hang the mirror (or prop it against the wall, if it's large enough) so that it catches and reflects the foyer light. Alternatively, you could hang metallic wallpaper in a foyer. The surface is subtly reflective, and it will give the whole space a more luminous appeal.

A FUNCTIONAL FOYER

A welcoming entry is not just clean and well lit, but it works well, too. How do you keep the clutter that you worked so hard to remove from building up again? And how do you make this part of your home as useful and friendly as possible? You need a system.

The system doesn't have to be complicated. Remember my grandmother's house? She had a wide, rustic bench that suited the style of her home and a big basket where we could toss our shoes and boots if they were wet. Her system was easy, and it kept things looking good.

If space in your entry allows, provide a bench or chair to sit down. This adds an element of comfort, and makes putting shoes on and taking them off easy. The bonus: When your family comes in they'll be more likely to get those shoes off right away, saving your floors.

ULTIMATE BOOT CAMP   FINDING JUST THE RIGHT LIGHT

If your foyer is dim or the light fixture is uninspired, go ahead and replace that light. It's possible to do this in less than a day, but I'd allow for a week so you have plenty of time to look around and find a fixture you love. You'll be seeing your entry in a new light in no time. Some things to keep in mind:

- **The size of a chandelier** or other hanging light should match your space. A tiny fixture dangling in the middle of a cavernous foyer looks silly, and a giant light in a cramped entry only makes it look more cramped. For my clients with large foyers, I always recommend they go grand: a big crystal chandelier adds incomparable sparkle and instant glamour. In a really large space, an additional lamp on a side table or console can have a pleasing, balancing effect. In a smaller space, go for a more petite pendant light. There are plenty of styles with tons of personality.

- **Go online for fun fixtures.** Browse online retailers and auction sites for lights that catch your eye. This is a great way to shop if you want to compare costs without sales pressure. Just be sure to check measurements carefully before placing an order.

- **For instant gratification,** try home improvement or lighting specialty stores. Ask to see only those fixtures available for immediate delivery. You can also score a distinctive fixture fast at your local flea market or antiques shop; just be prepared to make a stop at a hardware store for rewiring.

- **Don't forget to look around** your house! You might have a terrific table lamp gathering dust in the attic. A new shade might be all it needs to become the perfect, luminous accessory for an entry console table.

Entry furniture should enhance your home and make your life a bit easier, too. Here, a narrow console table is perfect for catching keys and other daily necessities, and the mirror lets you check your smile before heading out the door.

White walls don't have to be boring. Your entry can have tons of personality if you go bold with accessories. Here, a green armchair, a vase of purple hydrangeas, and a blue-patterned rug add color to a foyer, while an oversized abstract painting provides a dash of modern chic.

GET ORGANIZED, AND STAY THAT WAY

Keeping the entryway clutter-free is about establishing good habits and using a few tricks and accessories to help stay organized. You can find these things and install them in your foyer in a long weekend, and you'll have a great new look!

• **Install a console** with special trays or hooks for your keys. Avoid the temptation to let mail pile up here. Toss junk mail into recycling immediately,

and move the rest to a home office or other place for paperwork.

• **Make a new rule** for your family: no leaving shoes out. If you have a mudroom or other utility entrance, have them use that when their shoes are muddy or wet. In an all-purpose entry, put a special tray or basket on the floor of the coat closet to catch dirty shoes. Since guests will be wearing their shoes around the house,

be sure to have a good doormat outside and entry rug just inside the door for wiping feet.

• **Organize that coat closet.** Make sure there is adequate space for guest coats and hats, as well as your own. A trip to a home store will enlighten you about all the great storage options now available.

You'll also want a table or other spot that can serve to organize all the stuff that comes into the house every day. If you have piles of mail now, take a few minutes to sort it, and then create a new system to handle it going forward. I like to leave an "in-box" by the door that I sort daily, throwing away the junk mail and filing whatever needs to be saved, so there isn't a pileup.

If you're overwhelmed by this task, consider hiring a professional organizer to come and help. For a fee, this person will set up a system that works for your lifestyle.

GETTING CLEVER WITH COLOR

You're making progress in turning your entry into a welcoming, stylish space. Now the real fun begins—adding color. I love to see color in an entry. It does an amazing job of defining a space and instilling it with personality. Cheerful, warm hues beat out blah beiges any day. Color adds character and just make the space feel more inviting.

There are no firm rules about using color in the entry. If you want to try an intense shade in a small foyer, go for it. One of my clients has a tiny entry space, and she went bold with it, painting the walls turquoise and hanging an amber crystal chandelier. The intense color gives the little room more presence. It also creates an enticing through-the-rabbit-hole effect, which draws people through the entry and into the main living space. And it's a fabulous reflection of her style.

On the other hand, white can work, too. I generally avoid white in tiny entries, because this is just asking for dings on the walls from bags and packages as people go in and out. But if you have plenty of space, white can be the perfect blank canvas for bolder accessories, such as that Venetian mirror or a piece of colorful art. If your foyer is really large, white walls can look a bit cold. To make them work, you just need to go bigger and bolder with accessories. Don't be shy!

MINI BOOT CAMP FRESHEN UP THE FAMILY ENTRANCE

Lots of us actually have two entries in our homes: the formal front entry and the more casual family entrance. This might be a garage entrance, a back kitchen door, or a side door into a mudroom. It's easy for this space to become a sloppy catchall for whatever your family brings home, but remember that guests and potential buyers will probably see this area, too. So keep it organized and make sure everything has a place. The fastest solution is to run to a home-organization store and buy the supplies you need. You can easily accomplish this in a weekend. If you have a few extra days, you could also hire a professional organizer to create a system for you.

- **Unlike in the formal front** entry, you may keep shoes out here. Neatly. No piles. Buy a bin or basket and a metal tray to put wet or muddy boots.

- **Get a stand for umbrellas.** Look for one that will catch water, in case they're put away wet.

- **Install a series** of beautiful, ornamental hooks on the wall. (Not those cheap plastic ones.) These are great for keys, hats, and raincoats.

- **If you have the space,** perhaps on a wall-mounted shelf, buy a bin for each family member. There they can toss their gloves and scarves to keep them out of the way and easy to grab.

- **Kids' gear takes** some special accommodations. Consider designating a "parking area" for your stroller, just inside the door, and put a waterproof mat down in that spot to protect the floor from dirty, wet wheels. A large storage basket or two can corral sports equipment, but don't bring bikes inside— that's just asking for tire marks on the walls. They should go in the garage or basement if possible.

Feeling a bit wild? The entry is a small space, but you can make a big statement here with funky accessories, like this colorful, graphic rug and fruity chandelier. This side chair looks like it's smiling!

When contemplating color in the entry, think about the rooms that connect to it. If your house has an open plan and you can easily see the living room, dining area, kitchen, or other spaces from the foyer, you'll want to be sure that the colors in these spaces are harmonious and balanced visually.

The first apartment I owned had a dark narrow foyer. Because the space was self-contained and you couldn't see directly into other rooms from it, I decided to glam it up by painting it a Chinese lacquer red. I also hung a chandelier and an art-deco mirror and shelf.

This was the perfect solution to brighten up that dark space and to make it more useful. And since it was separated from the main rooms of the home, I could go for a vibrant painting treatment.

On the other hand, my client Caroline's foyer opened directly into the rest of her house and set the tone for the whole house the moment anyone stepped inside the entryway. When guests arrived, they entered a room that we had furnished with a table, two lamps, and a white orchid. The walls were painted with wide, horizontal black-and-white stripes. The look was bold, but classic, and it worked beautifully with her modern home.

FOYER FURNITURE SHOPPING

The right furniture is the key to great style and easy functionality in any foyer, large or small. If you're looking at an empty or poorly furnished entry, it's time to go shopping. Allow yourself a week for this if you can—you'll have time to browse and wait a few days for delivery if necessary. Some tips:

• **Look for pieces that suit your entry,** in both style and scale. In a tiny, modern apartment entrance or the all-purpose entry of a small house, you'll do best to choose a slim console or a petite demilune table and little else. In a large foyer, you can go much bigger and more luxe. Try a plush armchair in a formal, classic entry. Otherwise try a long bench, or sturdy pedestal table and side chair.

• **Start with basics,** and check out the big home-supply stores. They contain everyday staples, like doormats, console tables, and chairs.

• **Cast a wide net.** If you're looking for something really distinctive, browse online retailers and auction sites (where you can find beautiful reproduction and salvage pieces, as well as antiques), and wander through local antique stores and flea markets. You might snag an unusual side table, a classic Shaker bench, a gorgeous planter . . . possibilities abound.

• **Think beyond tradition.** Look for pieces that can do double duty in your entry, such as a tall bookcase that makes for a beautiful display while separating the foyer from an adjacent room. A secretary-style desk is a nice solution for an entry, since it offers both storage and good looks, and there are styles, from prim vintage pieces to sleek modern ones, to complement any setting.

• **Don't forget to add a mirror.** Hang it on the wall, or place it atop a console table. It will brighten and open the space and let you do a last check (and remind yourself to smile!) before you head out the door. The style can be simple or ornate, modern or vintage; choose what you love.

As much as I love bold color, I think it has its place. A dramatic, deeply saturated hue like kelly green or sunshine yellow in the entry will look awkward against a muted, earthy living room color scheme. You don't want your foyer to look like a guest who showed up in a clown costume for an elegant dinner party.

If your entry opens right into other rooms, you can use color to help define the space, but make sure the style is consistent so the look isn't jarring. If you're going for a chic, urban vibe, try rich espresso tones; in a modern setting with lots of white, try splashes of vivid red; in a Scandinavian-style home, go for calming grays.

Choose a fixture that suits not only the scale but also the style of your foyer. This glass pendant light has a lantern-like quality, making it right at home in this rustic entryway.

"STYLE IS KNOWING WHO YOU ARE, WHAT YOU WANT TO SAY, AND NOT GIVING A DAMN."

—GORE VIDAL

2. A Living Room for All Occasions

The living room is a major hub in the home. While your entry might be all about first impressions, this room makes a lasting impact. When you entertain, the living room is your showplace. And the last thing you want is a saggy sofa or messy bookshelves ruining the scene.

Whenever I work with a client, I make this room a priority. Whether the goal is to sell the house or just to set the mood for a festive holiday party, it's essential that everything looks and feels good. This certainly does not mean having everything perfect. The living room simply needs to feel comfy and inviting. Perfectionists not allowed!

Recently my husband and I went to a dinner party at the new home of our friends Jeanne and Benjamin. Their furniture hadn't arrived yet, but that didn't prevent them from entertaining. They created a fun atmosphere by creatively stacking encyclopedias under a red painted door for a sofa then layering on cushions and throw pillows so it was soft and relaxing. A plush rug defined the seating area, and the impromptu "sofa" anchored it at one end. A trunk became a coffee table, and the floor was covered with more cushions. They played a groovy soundtrack, served delicious food, and had candles flickering around the room. The mood was instant fun.

There is no need to delay inviting friends over and loving the room you have now. Be creative and make the best with the things you already own.

The living room in a New York City apartment is a gathering spot and a showplace for favorite things. Here, a plush sofa and sculptural glass-topped coffee table invite lingering, and artwork collected from friends makes a statement.

A SPACE TO ENJOY TOGETHER

Of course, on a day-to-day basis, you also want your living room to be a place where you feel comfortable, well, living. This might be your only common, quiet space, where one person may sit and read while another knits, and two others play Scrabble®. A successful living room is suited to entertaining as well as nesting and should have the versatility to transition easily between these roles.

As you might expect, there are some obstacles to achieving a room like that. Here are some of the common living room challenges that I see:

- The room feels chaotic and cluttered rather than calm and inviting.
- The style of the room needs updating, thanks to hand-me-down sofas, side tables, and other outdated pieces.
- Furniture arrangement is heavy and awkward and doesn't facilitate changing needs.
- There's an intangible feeling in the room that keeps it from being as comfortable as it should be. This might stem from improper lighting, a blah color scheme, or a lack of texture and softness.

But here's the good news. There are quick, easy fixes that will have you loving your living room faster than you can slipcover a sofa. We'll begin by making sure that the "foundation" of the living room is in place and well positioned. By foundation, I mean the primary furnishings such as sofa, coffee table, side tables and chairs, and lighting. Then we'll discuss layering on accessories to reflect your sense of style and infuse the room with a comfortable, inviting personality.

What's important to remember (and this is a mantra in this book, so you'll be seeing it a lot), is that this is *speed* decorating. This isn't about hiring a professional decorator to make over your space or setting rigid guidelines about a long and involved process. It is not about throwing out every piece of furniture in the room to create a blank slate. This is about discovering your own "Inner Speed Decorator."

When you have objects that you love, it's easy to group them together. Here, a funky lamp we found at the flea market looks great with a platinum glazed vase on a Platner® side table.

It's important to be resourceful and creative. This discarded window now lights up our fireplace. I painted it canary yellow and wrote a quote from a poet I love on it. We found the chair at a flea market and reupholstered it in silk velvet.

49

There are many ways to update familiar living room furniture and inject energy into a room. This gorgeous suzani from Morocco and throw pillows in peacock hues give new life to a wonky sofa.

As I've said before, when you do this, you can evaluate your own room, determine priorities, and get to work making it the most beautiful space that it can be, fast.

Since this is about speed, it's critical to set a deadline. Need a quick refresher for tonight's cocktail party? I have ideas for you (see "Last-Minute Cocktail Party Prep," on page 55 for details). Maybe you have the luxury of a full week before guests arrive, to really reassess and update the space. In any case, I'll help you choose tasks that give the most wow factor in the time you have.

SKIP THE SLIPCOVER

Remember the three-step approach I explained at the beginning of the book? Evaluate the situation. Explore solutions. Take action. So, step one, take a good look at the living room and ask yourself if it's meeting your needs. What are the primary functions of the space? Does it suit them? While doing this, start to make a list of the changes you'd like to make as well as any repairs or housekeeping tasks that need attention.

When time is tight, you might be tempted to skip the evaluation step and rush headlong into making repairs or buying new things. This is a common mistake. I always say to my clients "Stop! Don't buy anything until we make a plan." In one instance, a client named Shelly called me because she wanted advice on a new coffee table. When I went to her house, I saw her living room packed with heavy, mismatched furniture. She had printed out several coffee table styles she'd found online and was determined to get a new one. She was looking for something with glass to lighten up the room.

After carefully considering the room, however, we decided to move the coffee table down the priority list. In order to lighten up the room, we first needed to reposition the piano, which was hogging all the floor space. We also needed to lighten up the heavily loaded bookcase. The lesson is this: Take the time now to step back and quietly contemplate what your room really needs and what you really want. You'll save yourself countless hours, cash, and much aggravation in the end.

Focus on the things you love about your room, and work on enhancing them. This fireplace brings warmth—literally and visually—and is a gorgeous focal point.

This room provides a busy family plenty of space for lounging and playful activities. The colorful sofas, side chairs, and tables create a relaxing and inspiring vibe.

LIVING ROOM CHALLENGES

Once you've identified your living room challenges, it's time to explore solutions. What you can accomplish depends on your time frame. Looking for the speediest way to breathe new life into your living room? Do a good cleaning and then edit your possessions, including cluttered bookshelves and tables scattered with knickknacks. It will take less than a day and make a dramatic difference. Similarly, you can rearrange furniture, add a few vibrant accessories, and even repaint in a day or a weekend.

Allow yourself a full week if you plan to shop for bigger ticket items such as a sofa or a new rug. This gives you more options and keeps you from feeling too rushed. Such a purchase is an investment, after all, and deserves some careful thought. Consider, too, that you might have to wait a few days for delivery. Of course, some furniture can take months to arrive—but with speed decorating, we'll limit our choices to items that are in stock and ready to deliver. Lucky for us, many fantastic items are available, so you can have instant gratification. Also, if you need to enlist a handyperson or electrician to install a new light or do a minor repair, it's nice to have a few days flexibility in your schedule.

On the pages that follow, we'll look at those big living room challenges: the clutter, the lack of style, the awkward furniture arrangement, and the vital details that are missing or out of place, such as lighting and personal touches. In each case, I'll show you the speed decorator's solutions.

Everything has its place. A sculptural bronze bowl, fresh flowers from the garden, and nature-inspired accessories enhance this rustic family room, and the vibrant hues of tangerine and grapefruit throw pillows add va-va-voom.

CLUTTER, CLUTTER EVERYWHERE

The living room is often a catchall for family activities, so it's no wonder that it ends up jumbled and messy. Keeping it tidy and organized is a common challenge. Fortunately, there's an easy solution: Get rid of the stuff! If you're a sentimental saver (or just a plain pack rat), force yourself to let go. I remember the very first clients I worked with—Jane and Henry. When I stepped into their home, I knew my work was cut out for me. In the living room a card table was set up as an impromptu dining table,

LAST-MINUTE COCKTAIL PARTY PREP

If you just decided to have some friends over tonight, you have to work fast.
Don't try to make every detail perfect. Just keep it simple.

1. **CLEAN UP THE CLUTTER;** hide all those stacks of papers.

2. **MAKE AN INSTANT SIDE TABLE:** Stack magazines neatly on the floor and top it with a bowl of nuts.

3. **MAKE SURFACES SHINE.** Spray and polish all mirrors and glass until they gleam.

4. **PUT OUT A VASE OF FRESH FLOWERS.**

5. **TURN DOWN THE LIGHTS,** and festoon the room with candles to light moments before the guests arrive.

because there wasn't a chance you could eat off the kitchen table, stacked as it was with mail and notebooks. Shelving units lined all the walls and were crammed with everything from freebie vases from the florist to Japanese scrolls, CDs, sheet music, and porcelain figures. Sickly plants convalesced near the window. Jane and Henry knew that something needed to be done but weren't sure what. They'd lived there for so long they didn't know how to begin getting rid of stuff. So that's where we began.

The more stuff you have lying around, the more claustrophobic and less welcoming your space feels. So before you even *think* of buying anything new, you have to get stripping. You might even find that once the room is clean and clear, you don't need so many new things after all.

Start with a Deep Clean

Never underestimate the power of a sparkling clean room. Hire a cleaning service or just put on your rubber gloves and do it yourself. Vacuum everywhere, including the chairs and sofas (and under their cushions); move furniture and vacuum underneath. Dust every surface, removing objects and books from shelves to get every nook and cranny; don't forget chair rails, baseboards, table legs, and lampshades. Clean all windows and windowsills. (See "Five Speed Cleaning Tips," page 11, for help getting this done fast.)

REVAMP YOUR COFFEE TABLE

Here's a quick refresher that will take you just a few hours:

- **BUY A NICE DECORATIVE BOWL** and fill it with fruit, or buy a vase and fill it with white tulips or peonies.

- **BUY (OR PULL FROM YOUR SHELVES)** two or three inspiring coffee table books of similar size and color and stack them.

- **REMOVE ANY OTHER CLUTTER,** and you have a fresh new look on the coffee table.

Take Stock

Remove items that are ugly, stained, or ripped. Sort items into areas or piles: keep it, get rid of it, fix it. Remove anything that isn't a "keep it" item from the room. Clear off table surfaces. Choose a few knickknacks and arrange them so they can be seen, and relocate or get rid of the rest. Make a note of any frayed wires or cracked plaster that require professional attention, and schedule repairs now.

Organize Bookshelves

Personally, I am very attached to my books. But editing a book collection can be freeing. Sort through and donate books you don't like or won't read again. Recycle old magazines. Mingle decorative items with the books for a more interesting display. (See "Mini Boot Camp: Create a Bombshell Bookcase," on page 59 for lots of great tips.)

A tall, built-in bookcase is a showcase for a collection of coral as well as a practical spot for books and electronics.

Collect Yourself

Collections are great fun, but an overgrown one can look more like a mess than a stylish reflection of your taste. Take the plunge and pare down a collection that has gotten out of control. If you have an abundance of china plates and serving platters, pick your favorites and arrange them on the wall using plate hangers to show them off. As for the rest, take photos to help you remember what you have and store them away. There's no rule that says you have to have everything out at once.

Of course there are ways not to display a collection. I'll never forget the first time I walked into the Whitman's living room. This was a family home, and yet this primary living space felt more like the Explorer's Club. Mr. Whitman's collection of spears, knives, guns, and other hunting weaponry covered the walls, along with tribal warrior masks from his adventures in Africa. A huge glass cabinet contained more of the same. An overwhelmed Mrs. Whitman wanted it gone. Since the house was going on the market soon, I had to agree with her.

Not wanting to force Mr. Whitman to part with his beloved collection entirely, I helped them come up with a gentler solution. We ended up turning a spare bedroom into a den, where he could display some (but not all!) of those items. The rest went into storage. The living room, now free of its hunt club theme, could be brightened with natural elements, such as orchids, and arranged for comfortable family living.

A STYLISH FOUNDATION

Once you've paired down, you can think about how and what to add. This can be a particular challenge in the living room since this is your most public space and the choices are so varied. But remember that this is the room to invest in the basics. If you purchase a great-quality sofa, side tables, coffee table, and elegant light fixtures, you'll create a solid foundation that you can keep for many years. And you can always make them new again with throw pillows, decorative accessories, and other "temporary" items.

Before you splurge on those investment pieces, you'll want to have a good sense of your style. Defining it simply takes a little exploring. When I met Sara for the first time, I was impressed with her sense of personal style—metallic flats, classic white shirt, funky belt, and a Marc Jacobs purse. Her furniture style, by contrast, was straight from the '80s. She had a collection of mostly hand-me-downs, and she just didn't know where to begin in furnishing her home to make it her own.

I suggested she start by looking through maga-zines to see what appealed to her. Inspiration can come from many places. We discussed what her favor-ite movies were, her dreams, her goals, her favorite vacation places, and how she wanted to feel in her home. Before long, Sara came up with a look for her living room.

CREATE A BOMBSHELL BOOKCASE

Have a free weekend? Dive into this project and give a bookcase—and your living room—a whole new look.

- **Remove boxes,** paper, photos, and other non-book items. Weed out old books that you don't like and donate to charity.

- **Neatly arrange your edited book collection.** Vary the arrangement—horizontal and vertical—of books for a pleasing display. I like to remove the book jackets and organize the books by spine color. Just slip the jackets behind the books on the shelves so they aren't damaged or lost. Stack magazines horizontally for a neater look.

- **Add small vases, seashells, sculpture,** artwork, and photos to break up the rows of books. But don't overdo it or you'll end up with more clutter.

- **Install spotlights** to illuminate the shelves, and string rope lighting along the top for instant ambience. Plug the lights into a timer and run an extension cord down the wall behind the unit, and along the baseboard to an outlet. Choose extension cord colors that will blend with the wall and molding colors for easy camouflage.

- **If you want a more dramatic makeover,** consider removing everything and painting your shelves a high-gloss white. Then lacquer the back panels in a bold hue, like poppy red. This will create depth and will really grab the eye.

●● A NOTE ABOUT ART

If you have posters hanging on your walls, pull them down and replace with original art or family photos. Those Monet water lily posters give your space more of a college-dorm look than that of a grown-up room. For a great twist on framed photos, you can have a picture you love printed out in large format at your local copy center or search the Internet for an online printing resource.

You could even take a photo of your favorite tree and then have it blown up for your living room. You might find that working on a speed decorating project inspires you to start a new collection. It's always a good time to make a first purchase. Two of my favorites are Swedish glassware and original art. My husband and I buy art to support our friends and fill our home with things we love.

Here was the foundation: She liked shiny things, so we found light fixtures with polished nickel bases. A classic white faux-suede sofa and a cowhide rug complemented them and grounded the room. Since she couldn't find a side table she liked, we stacked her favorite art books and magazines to anchor the sofa and placed a table lamp on one side. For texture, we added pillows in linen and velvet and a cashmere throw.

Finding your style might sound like slow, onerous project. But it doesn't have to be. Speed decorating can help you make the leap from confused to confident.

Go back to "Speedy Ways to Find Your Style," on page 13, and review the steps outlined there. Look at the clippings you gathered in your Speed Toolbox for inspiration. Mull over the furnishings you already own and the style and size of your home. Faster than you think, you'll find that patterns emerge. You probably already know, instinctively, what you love. Now is the time to embrace those things and forge ahead.

MAKING YOUR FURNITURE WORK

Once you have the right foundation pieces, you're on your way to great style. But proper arrangement of those pieces is what will make your room comfortable and inviting. A living room is for living, after all. And how do we live in it? We gather, we snack, we chat, we play games. We want places to lounge and relax that are conducive to those activities. But the biggest and most common mistake that people make in a living room is to push everything up against the walls, leaving a "doughnut" in the middle. This arrangement just results in unusable empty space, which isn't conducive to anything.

Recently I was working on a project for a family, and, sure enough, they had all their living room furniture smashed against the walls. The room was small, and they were clearly trying to make it seem bigger with this arrangement. But it actually felt crowded and awkward.

●●● SUBTRACT BEFORE YOU ADD

What you take away from a room can be just as important in establishing style as what you add. If you inherited furnishings that don't suit your tastes, or if you moved into a new home with a style very different from your last and some of your belongings just don't "fit," it's time to make a change.

I once gave this advice to a client of mine named Tom, a bachelor whose living room was defined by a large, green and mauve, floral print rug. He had inherited it from his mother. All he needed to do was roll up that rug and haul it away. With the wood floor revealed, the room instantly had a more masculine appeal.

This rattan hanging egg chair and ottoman create a cozy reading nook. Books arranged by color, such as these white-spined volumes, make an artistic and functional display.

SPEEDY WAYS TO DEFINE YOUR SPACE

- **Pull the furniture away** from the wall to allow it to breathe. You don't have to put the sofa in the middle of the room—just a few inches will make the space less crowded visually.

- **Think of furniture arrangement** in terms of groupings: a few pieces that relate to one another and create distinct spaces for activities like conversation, reading, or writing a letter. You can have multiple groupings in one room. This will create walkways and add functionality.

- **Choose chairs, ottomans,** and side tables that are easy to pick up and move by one person. These are great for accommodating movement for various needs, such as pulling a chair over to another grouping to join a conversation or card game.

- **Use area rugs to your advantage:** Do not cover an entire floor, but rather use them to pull together a seating area or another distinct space in the room.

Furniture, just like people, needs a little "personal space" so it can breathe. I suggested moving the sofa just six inches from the wall to give it that space. We then positioned the coffee table, side chair, end table, and lamps near the sofa to create a grouping. This provided a comfortable conversation area. A side table and a stack of books flanked the chair, so it was also a space in itself for reading or other quiet activities. Finally, I suggested we replace the rug, which was too big, with a smaller area rug. That helped define the conversation area and made the whole room feel bigger.

In thinking about good arrangement, especially from a speed decorator's point of view, details count. Pay attention to the smaller pieces of furniture that you use to fill out and accessorize the room. Stools, side chairs, and benches should be versatile and easy to move around.

Lightweight side tables can hold lamps and decorative items but are also easy to move for a spontaneous supper on the sofa.

Smart arrangements, including the placement of rugs, can help you carve out spaces for activities in your home. Here, a zebra rug layered over a sisal rug helps define the TV-viewing area.

●●● A NOTE ABOUT THE TELEVISION

Does the TV really belong in the living room? This room is all about connecting with friends and family. To prevent it from turning into a noisy viewing gallery, it's ideal to have a separate media room or family room where you keep the television. If you can't do that, or don't want to, then there are some rules to make the TV presentable:

- **Arrange seating** so the priority is conversation. The TV should not be the focal point. This is still your living room, not a movie theater, so don't sacrifice those conversation areas.

- **Get rid of the big clunky television** and invest in a flat panel model. These are less obtrusive and look great.

- **Control the tangle of cords** behind the TV—keep them bundled with zip ties and out of sight.

- **Optional:** When guests arrive, make the TV part of the ambience by playing one of those DVDs with the yuletide fire burning or a fish tank in the summer.

- **Put the TV on (or in) an attractive media center.** There's no need to buy an enormous armoire to hide the unit away completely, especially if your living room is small. There are many good-looking, stylish ways to go, such as placing the flat screen on a sideboard like the ones featured here. One is modern, the other is white lacquered. Or you can hang it over the fireplace.

A striped armchair can be pulled around for movie watching or aside for quiet reading.

●●● FURNITURE THAT DOES DOUBLE DUTY

Items like stools and ottomans that serve more than one purpose are a speed decorator's friend. They make the room look good, and create versatility to switch from the everyday, to Super Bowl party, or to evening cocktails with ease.

I once had a client, Roger, whose living room was the ultimate "guy space." He had a small dining table in the living room, equipped with a hot plate, toaster, and coffee maker, so he could easily cook and eat without leaving the room. To give the room a more grown-up, entertaining-friendly style, we put the kitchen items where they belonged, in the kitchen, and got rid of that table. Instead, we bought two leather cubes and a nice serving tray. The cubes functioned as ottomans for kicking back and putting up feet, but also held the tray for the occasional TV dinner. The same cubes become extra seating when guests arrive.

LET THERE BE LIGHT

Few people realize how vital good lighting is to the comfort and utility of a room. The truth is, you can have a sparkling clean, well-arranged, stylish room and if it's not well lit, the effect will be lost. It's important not only to have enough light but flattering, comfortable light that is correctly placed.

Recently I visited a family who had just moved into a modern home after many years living in a traditional one. They had purchased halogen floor lamps for the living room, but those only served to cast harsh light in the corners. The room didn't feel inviting at all. Since they wanted it to be a cozy gathering spot, we got rid of those lights and looked at what else they had in their collection. They already owned a charming, arching floor lamp that wasn't in use. We placed that in the center of the room and the effect was instant: warm and welcoming.

FIVE TIME- AND EFFORT-SAVING TIPS FROM A FURNITURE-MOVING VETERAN

1. **Get Magic Sliders®:** These products, a bit larger than a kitchen sponge, make moving heavy furniture a breeze. There are two versions available, one for carpet, in a hard plastic with foam on the back, and one for hardwood, in fuzzy wool. Just stick them under the feet of a table or a sofa, and it will zip across the floor, especially useful if you want to try out your sofa in several spots.

2. **Make creative use of rug pads:** To keep your sofa or other piece of furniture from slipping and sliding when you sit down, a quick thing to do is cut a rug pad into pieces the size of the legs and slip them underneath. The sofa will stay in place and the floors won't be scratched.

3. **Add felt pads to furniture feet:** These fuzzy wool buttons come in a wide range of sizes at housewares stores.

They are sticky on one side so they adhere to your furniture. The protective pads keep your hardwood floors flawless.

4. **Borrow a little muscle:** Look online for a furniture lifter (I like to call it "Mr. Man"). It's about a foot long and looks like a boomerang. Slide it under a heavy piece of furniture like an armoire, and you have instant leverage to lift it. Then you can easily put a slider underneath to move the piece.

5. **Erase those dents:** You know those ugly marks left behind in the rug after you move a piece of furniture? You can get rid of them with some plain old ice cubes. Just place some ice in each dent, and let it melt. The fibers will loosen, and you can then fluff them up with your fingers, a wide-tooth comb, or even a fork.

Aside from setting a mood, use light to help define distinct spaces in a room. You need ambient light, which is soft and makes everyone look good. But task lighting—whether for that game of chess or the book of poetry you're reading—is important, too.

Here are some ways to make the most of your living room lights.

Brighten the Bookcase

Use well-placed lights to transform a dark, heavy bookcase into a pleasing display. Spotlights installed into the top of a bookcase will illuminate books and objets d'art. You can also hide rope lighting along the top, for a festive glow. Luxuriate in your chaise lounge and read. (For more details, see "Create a Bombshell Bookcase," on page 59.)

Hang a Chandelier

These more formal fixtures will brighten up a seating area. Hang one over a sofa and install a dimmer switch for light that can be bright and cheerful or soft and romantic, depending on what's going on. An electrician or handyperson can easily swap a chandelier for an existing ceiling fixture; if there isn't an existing one, you can simply hang the light from a hook, and swag the cord to a corner and run it down the wall to the nearest outlet.

Light fixtures aren't the only way to brighten a room. Window treatments let natural light in. The pale sofa and mohair blanket help to create an airy space.

Good lighting is essential to a comfortable living room. Here, sconces and floor lamp supplement the flood of daylight. A fireplace provides a cozy glow on cool evenings.

Details make a room. Here, a tall vase of branches by the fireplace, a log used as a side table, and a coral collection create a relaxing, woodsy mood. A soft throw on an armchair is a cozy touch.

Add Elegant Table Lamps

A sophisticated table lamp with a crisp clean shade creates a calm, relaxed feeling and casts a pleasant ambient light that's also bright enough to read or work by. Don't torture your light fixtures by making them wear uptight shades festooned with bright colors, ruffles, and pleats.

THE DETAILS THAT COUNT: TEXTURE, COLOR, AND PERSONAL TOUCHES

Once your furniture is in place and your lighting is right, it's time to start having fun in the living room. Adding warm, soft details like cozy textiles and throw pillows will make your room more comfortable and inviting. Accessories like vases of flowers and other natural elements can bring an infusion of life to the room, along with a sense of your personality. All of these pieces offer an opportunity to go for it style-wise. They are easy to swap in and out as your mood or the seasons change.

What's more, these easily changed details offer a chance to play with color. If your room is monochromatic and just kind of blah, a few colorful accessories can offer a revitalizing update. And once you add them, you might find you want to take a bolder step and repaint the room altogether.

Remember Roger, my client with the kitchen in his living room? Once we cleared out all the unnecessary items, we realized his space was in need of some personality. We decided to balance a heavy armoire that he had pushed against one

continued on p. 74

A sheepskin floor pillow offers a soft resting place on the hardwood floor and invites guests to get comfortable.

FOCUS ON THE FIREPLACE

A fireplace is the best way to create both light and warmth in the living room. Even if yours is nonworking, there are ways to enhance it and to use it as a light source rather than let it become a dark hole in a room. Some of the ideas here might take you a few days to a week; others just a few minutes!

Once I had a client who complained about the light in his living room. There were adequate windows and natural light and, yet, everything was a little off-kilter. The culprit was easy to find—a fireplace that didn't work was filled with books and papers like an extra storage cubby. There were votive candles on the wall next to the fireplace and a task lamp on the mantel. The light was in all the wrong places. We cleared up the clutter and placed white pillar candles in the fireplace for a soft, ambient glow.

You can use your fireplace to brighten your living room and amp up its style. Here are some ideas:

- **If you have a working fireplace,** the fall and winter are the perfect times to stoke it up. Even if you don't have time to chop and haul wood, you can use Duraflame® logs. Or look for Java-Logs® (carried by gourmet grocery stores), which are made from coffee grounds and burn cheerily. Whatever you do, keep it burning. Remember, the easy, speedy way to light a fire is to use a long-handled propane lighter. Don't mess around with matches or you'll just end up with burned fingers.

- **I often like to toss a few pinecones** into the fire for a woodsy aroma. You can buy sticks of fatwood or hickory chips, too, which give off a great fragrance.

- **In a nonworking fireplace, light candles!** It's fast and cozy to cluster candles in the hearth and light them. When filling a fireplace with candles, pick white pillars in various heights ranging from 6 inch to 12 inch. Cluster them in odd numbers, such as five or seven. This will create harmony and balance.

- **Convert your gas fireplace** to a wood-burning one. There are quite a few gas options on the market, but I rarely advise clients to use them. The ones that require the running of gas lines are the antithesis of speed decorating, and even those that don't still leave me cold. They lack the authentic feeling, warmth, crackling, and scent of real fire. It's a very simple procedure to convert it. Look up a professional in your phone book and they'll do their magic in a couple hours.

- **In wintertime, you can use your firewood** as an art installation. Have a cord (or a half cord) delivered to your home and stacked outdoors. Then bring some of that inside and stack it high, cut ends facing out, along the wall next to the hearth. It's handy and good looking. Just be sure to buy treated wood so you don't end up with pests.

- **In warmer weather, invest in a few white birch logs** and leave them in the fireplace. Their color will give the illusion of lightening the space rather than leaving it bare and dark.

A few adored pieces, well placed, can add tons of personality to a room. The painted ceramic owl and Scandinavian candlesticks make a chic display.

This colorful ceramic table lamp dresses up a set of nesting side tables. Other fun details include personalized coasters and an enameled box, which is a great place to stash a remote control or candy.

wall by placing a bamboo plant in the corner. On the other side, we placed a single white orchid on a side table. Because the room was filled with brown leather, we bought some red throw pillows along with the red serving tray. A gourd-shaped ceramic vase filled with white lilies was a final detail that also helped brighten the dark room. The effect was charming, still masculine, but it looked as if someone lived there who really cared about the space.

Here are some no-fail ways to personalize the living room.

Stock Up on Vases for Natural Displays

Swedish glass is fun for a pop of color. Or buy ceramic containers in one color like white or cream in various shades and shapes and cluster them in groups of three or five. Odd numbers look best.

Pile on the Pillows

Layer throw pillows on the sofa to add color. Floor pillows provide extra comfy seating. I love velvet pillows, in particular, which bring an instant feeling of elegance and comfort.

A NEW PAINT JOB

Fresh paint is one of the best and easiest ways to bring a living room back to life. It's good to take a few days to a week for this, so you have time to mull over colors, try test patches, and wait for each coat to dry. Some guidelines:

- **Go for a new color scheme.** You can do something calming with natural colors or get a little wild (as nature does) with bursts of red or orange. I also love warm gray tones.

- **Apply test patches,** at least 2 feet by 2 feet in size, and examine them in different lights, at different times in the day, before deciding on one color. Many paint companies sell colors in sample sizes for this purpose. Alternatively, you can get oversized paint chips and hang them for the same effect.

- **Start with clean walls** and patch and prime first. If you're going for a bold color that requires several coats, like deep red, get a tinted primer to make the job go faster.

- **Add accessories,** such as throw pillows, to complement your new color scheme.

Add a Throw

A creamy cashmere throw is the perfect way to bring warmth into a room. For a splash of color, pick something fun like shocking pink mohair. If you're going for a classic look try herringbone cashmere.

Find the Right Rug

I always use these selections because they're typically available off-the-shelf and they come in a variety of sizes: Natural fiber rugs such as jute are a great all-purpose way to go. Flokati rugs feel great and make the room feel cozy. Cowhide rugs and sheepskin rugs are great choices, too. Toss sheepskin rugs on the floor or use on a chair for extra softness.

Accessories from other rooms might find a new home in the living room. This cozy throw is just the thing to complete a well-loved armchair. A stack of books makes the perfect sidetable.

PLAYING UP YOUR BEST FEATURES

This chapter has suggestions of things to add that will bring style, softness, and charm to your living room. But before you launch into shopping, it's smart to take a closer look at the items you already own. Chances are there are treasures waiting to be rediscovered!

One of the most effective ways of evaluating the accessories and fixtures is by taking them all out of the room and looking at them out of context. You can objectively decide what you like and put those pieces back in a new way. This is also a great time to repair any torn upholstery or light fixtures with frayed wires. The pieces you don't like—or damaged beyond repair—should be donated or tossed.

Your own treasures and personal touches are what make your home really YOU. Here, an eclectic mix of furniture, accessories, and objets d'art gives this living room charming, comfortable family style.

●●● CORRALLING THE CORDS

When placing lamps in strategic spots or running rope lights along a shelf, you'll find that an electrical outlet isn't always where you need it. This is where extension cords come in. Fortunately, it's easy to keep them from becoming a tangled mess.

- **Whenever possible, run the cord** to the nearest corner, then down the corner wall where it will be least noticeable. Likewise, at floor level, run it along the baseboard so it blends.

- **Use wire molding** to cover the cords and paint the molding the color of the wall.

- **The quickest way** to bind several cords together is to use zip ties. You can get them at the hardware store in a color that matches the cords. Velcro® strips are similarly effective. Many gadgets abound for this purpose, but I find them unwieldy and unnecessary.

- **If running cords** for lights along the tops of cabinets or book-shelves, consider adding a piece of crown molding at the top: This creates a lip that hides those cords.

- **Use Velcro strips** or tape to attach cords to the backs of tables or shelves against a wall so they don't bunch up at floor level.

Assess Accessories

Pick a neutral spot where the lighting is good and assemble all your vases, pillows, throws, throw rugs, plants, flowers, artwork, and so on. To do the most thorough job, pull not only from the living room but from other rooms as well. Group them by type and color, and evaluate each piece. If you decide you'd like a new color palette, you don't have to replace everything. For pillows, you can simply buy (or make, if you're handy with a sewing machine) new slipcovers.

Do a Lamp Lineup

Just as with accessories, you can gather all your table and floor lamps in one place and look them over. Out of their usual context, you might see them in a new light.

You might discover that the very lamp you need for your living room has been lurking in the bedroom all along. Likewise, check your attic or basement for lamps that have been languishing because of things like faulty wiring or a damaged shade—such things are easy to fix and cost hardly a thing. Also this is a great time to purge—get rid of the lamps you don't like. Just because they're working doesn't mean you need to hang on to them. Free yourself of the guilt—donate them and let someone else make good use of them.

If you have an old lamp in a style that no longer fits your home, a quick make-over might be all it needs. The key is to look at the lamp base: If its fundamental shape and size is acceptable, most everything else is fixable. If it needs rewiring, a quick trip to your local hardware store will yield the supplies and help you need.

A lamp can make a stylish statement, as well as provide a source of light, as with this large metal Paul Evans lamp. The coffee table here was found at a railroad yard—it can handle wear and tear in a bustling family room.

3. The Cook's Kitchen

My approach to the kitchen couldn't be simpler. Make it as welcoming and user-friendly as possible, and have fun. When it comes to decorating this room, you want it to be stylish and comfortable for guests, since invariably, people will gravitate there.

Whenever my husband and I have guests over, somehow everyone ends up gathering in our tiny kitchen, talking and drinking. It doesn't matter that it's cramped. People love to hang out and catch up as I'm taking hors d'oeuvres out of the oven or chopping vegetables.

Since this rule seems to hold true everywhere, it always pays to be sure your kitchen looks its best. Even when you have a dinner party under way and cook up a storm, the space should be comfortable and presentable.

I also emphasize the kitchen for my clients who are selling their homes. If you're having an open house, you want to make sure that the kitchen is inspiring. When people walk in and see the room, they should feel like they want to entertain there.

Of course, on a day-to-day basis, having a kitchen that's clean and comfortable just makes sense. This is where you cook and eat every day, so it has to be functional and easy to work in. It has to be versatile, not only for cooking but also for settling down with your laptop and browsing recipes or answering email. It has to be clean, for your health's sake.

And since you spend a lot of time here, the way it looks should make you happy. If you've been living with a tired, outdated kitchen, just think of the pleasure you will have making your morning coffee every day in a room that is cheerful and attractive.

A comfortable, welcoming kitchen is a beautiful thing. Fresh flowers, a bowl of fruit, and colorful accents create a lively, warm scene.

What makes a kitchen a pleasure to use every day? Great light, ample workspace, and fun personal touches, such as this green subway tile backsplash and the vases of ornamental cabbages and tall peashoots.

Here are the most common kitchen decorating issues that I see:

- **There's too much clutter.** Countertops are loaded with appliances, there's no room to work, and the space is hard to keep clean.
- **The room is style challenged.** The cabinets, color scheme, flooring, and other details are outdated and tired.
- **It isn't accommodating.** There isn't enough seating for guests, or what's there is awkward rather than inviting.
- **It just doesn't work.** The space isn't arranged so you can quickly move from stove to sink to refrigerator to counter workspace, and the lighting is poor.

If your kitchen is suffering from some of these problems, or even all of them, rest assured that there are quick solutions available. It's time to take action and create a kitchen that works for you.

Feeling overwhelmed? Don't fret. Many people get dizzy at the prospect of making changes in their kitchens. They see it as an all-or-nothing proposition. Renovate, move, or live with it in its tattered condition. But remember, the essence of speed decorating is fixing what is fixable and learning to love the rest. You might want to tear everything out, from floor tiles to plumbing, but you don't have to. In this chapter, we'll focus on giving your kitchen a fast update that really makes a difference.

TAKING STOCK

It might seem counterintuitive, but as I've explained before, speed decorating begins by slowing down. Just knowing that you don't like your kitchen table or wall color isn't enough. Take some time to look around and think about what your needs are in the room. Identify the problem areas and your priorities for fixing them before you start making changes.

A thoughtful evaluation process helps any speed decorator hone her game plan. Take Jane, for example. When I first met with her, she told me there was almost nothing she liked about her cramped, galley-style kitchen. She had a toddler and another child on the way and didn't have the money for a big renovation. She didn't know where to begin.

The first thing I suggested was that she list all the things she didn't like about the room. The list was long. It included ugly floor tile, not enough storage space, and dated, out-of-style cabinets. She also complained of an overall dull mood in the room, thanks to a beige color scheme.

Overall, it was a lot to address in the time we had. But with some careful planning, we came up with fast, doable solutions to address her immediate needs. We added storage and used paint and new cabinet doors to brighten and update the space. Those changes made a huge difference, and after they were in place, Jane and her family loved her new kitchen.

Comfortable seating is a must. This nook, with a bench upholstered in easy-to-clean green vinyl wrapping around a sturdy pedestal table, invites lounging and lingering over morning coffee.

Gut renovation not required. Details like a bold backsplash in red tile, a clean white Corian® countertop, and under-cabinet task lighting, can make a dramatic difference.

The Timeline

As with every other room in the house, how much decorating you can do in the kitchen depends on how much time you have. One day is enough time to clean the room thoroughly and remove clutter. You can also add colorful accessories in a day or less and even install some new lights, especially those that don't require drilling and rewiring.

In a long weekend, you can replace the kitchen faucet, repaint the room, or even reface the cabinets and update their hardware.

Bigger projects, such as putting in new flooring, can be done in a week's time, if you have help available and choose your materials carefully. A week is also enough time to shop for a new table and chairs or other furniture and allow for a few days' delivery time. If you need to recruit outside help for your projects, whether it's a plumber to put in a new sink, an electrician to hardwire a light fixture, or a handyperson to help refinish a floor, it's smart to allow a few days to a week.

Whatever projects you decide on, the deadline is crucial. I find it's the best motivator for getting work done. Maybe your mother-in-law is arriving this evening, or your real estate agent will be stopping by in two days. But if you don't already have a deadline looming, set one. For the kitchen, there's no better deadline than having a dinner party. Why not schedule one now for next week? Call some friends and invite them to christen your "new" room with a meal. Boom—you're locked in. Then get to work.

A CLEAN KITCHEN IS A HAPPY KITCHEN

The first thing I look for when I walk into a client's kitchen is cleanliness. Clean, clutter-free surfaces are essential for a kitchen that feels inviting. From a food-safety standpoint, you want to keep your work surfaces clean and sanitized. Paring down on all the stuff that accumulates on the counters, such as small appliances and spice jars, makes cleaning go easier and more quickly. It also looks better.

If you keep surfaces clear, of course, you'll always have a spot to cook and to eat. And as a bonus, a clean space makes up for many faults. If your guests see a sink that shines and a floor that's sparkling clean, they won't be so quick to notice that old, cream-colored refrigerator or the dings in the linoleum. Or at least, they won't be so quick to care.

A sparkling clean kitchen makes the best impression. Here, the floor and stainless steel stove gleam from polishing, and the lack of wall cabinets contributes to the open, fresh feeling.

A FRESH KITCHEN, FAST

If you have a day or less to get your kitchen into make-mom-proud shape, follow these steps:

- **CLEAR AWAY THE CLUTTER.** Relocate items that don't belong on the countertop. Clear the fridge of excess menus, art projects, photos, and magnets. Also, don't fall into the trap of using the top of your refrigerator as a storage spot. Put away those cereal boxes and bags of chips and replace them with one nice tray.

- **DO A DEEP CLEAN.** Get all surfaces, from floor to walls, using organic, nontoxic products. Remember that periodic deep cleans are vital to the speed decorator. Later, when guests are about to arrive, you can get by with a quick wipe of counters and sink.

- **HANG FRESH TOWELS.** Get into the habit of replacing hand and dish towels regularly. It looks better and is more sanitary, too.

- **DO A QUICK FOOD INVENTORY.** Sort through the items in the refrigerator and cabinets and throw out any food that is starting to spoil or products that are expired or that you haven't used in months. Place a bowl of fresh, beautiful fruit on the countertop.

- **ADD SOME FRAGRANCE.** A clean kitchen will smell good. But to make it even more appealing, simmer some mulling spices or pop some slice-and-bake cookies in the oven just before guests arrive.

A STYLE UPDATE

A clean kitchen is wonderful, but if you want to make a good impression on your guests, the style needs to be fresh, too. Maybe you're living with a kitchen that feels locked in a time warp, and the year is, say, 1972. Or perhaps you're just stuck with the bland laminate cabinets and generic neutral floor tiles that your builder installed. Either way, it's time for a change!

Update Your Cabinets

Without a doubt, cabinets have greater visual impact in the kitchen than nearly any other detail. Replacing them altogether is an expensive proposition. It's also a time-consuming one, so not a part of speed decorating. But you can give the cabinets you have a makeover. If they're a dreary color or a wood-grain laminate, a few coats

continued on p. 91

MAX OUT YOUR STORAGE

Part of having a comfortable, workable kitchen is having all the tools and supplies you need close by but not piling up all over your workspace. Expanding limited storage space is a great long-weekend project. Here are some tips:

- **Buy some plate racks.** These inexpensive, corner-shaped organizers tuck inside cabinets and allow you to stack your plates upright. This makes them easy to grab, and takes little room. I have them in my own cupboards.

- **Add extra shelves.** Organizing stores sell shelves made of plastic-coated wire or stainless steel that slide right into cabinets. Buy some, and use them to add another layer of vertical space. Arrange glasses on top and stack bowls beneath. They double your space.

- **Look beyond traditional cabinetry.** If you have the space, bring in a beautiful étagère or bookshelf to organize and display dishware, bowls, and vases.

- **Use magnets.** Rather than taking up cupboard space with spices and seasonings, get a bunch of magnetic spice jars and stick them right on the side of the refrigerator. They save space and look good. They help to keep the counters clear and keep your spices within easy reach.

- **Gather your recipes.** Buy a binder and organize all your magazine clippings and recipe cards in it. Or better yet, create an electronic recipe book and ditch the paper altogether.

Limit countertop items to a few beautiful and practical pieces, like this glass jar housing colorful peppers.

A lacquered red étagère makes a striking focal point in the corner of a kitchen and turns ordinary bowls and candlesticks into objets d'art.

Storage spaces are practical, but they can also be your kitchen's best style asset. Here, lower level cabinets and a generously pro-portioned island combine with open shelving above.

Modern, flat-paneled cabinet doors and metal hardware com-plement this contem-porary kitchen.

of paint can make a huge difference. Since different materials require different fin-ishes, I recommend paying a visit to your local home improvement or paint-supply store for advice on the right primer and paint to use for your cabinet surface.

Another thing you can do is remove and replace the cabinet doors altogether. If you have doors in an outdated, beveled style, take them down and buy simple, flat-fronted doors. Painted in a glossy shade, these will look modern and fresh. If you like the basic frame of your cabinets, you might just remove the doors alto-gether on the upper cabinets to create open storage. Paint the interior a bright color to create a cheerful display space for your dishes.

Add Color

For a speed decorator, the best tool for injecting instant style into a room is color. Don't be afraid of a vivid hue. Paint, after all, is easy enough to fix. You might start with one bold color on an accent wall, such as tomato red in a white or pale yellow kitchen, for instance. What a difference one wall can make. You'll see your room instantly come to life. You can add style to a kitchen in many ways beyond just paint, of course. The accessories, the floor, and even the appliances offer stylish opportunities.

What's the fastest way to bring your kitchen up to date? Color. A seaside blue color revitalized these flat-paneled cabinets, and vibrant accessories such as red dinner plates and a portrait of a cardinal add plenty of pop.

Vintage floor grates that suit the style of the house (here Victorian and Dutch Colonial, respectively) are an authentic touch.

A decorative hinge makes a graphic statement on an ordinary kitchen.

Etched, vintage metal pulls elevate simple white drawer fronts and coordinate well with a stone countertop.

Accessorize

Go out and buy a new teakettle, set of dish towels, and a wall clock. Pick cheerful colors that contrast with the basic color scheme of the room, so they'll stand out. Sometimes just a few little pops of color are all you need to bring a room to life.

Replace Your Hardware

If the cabinet knobs, drawer pulls, hinges, or even floor grates are dated and brassy, install new ones. You can easily do this in a single day. There are tons of styles available, from shiny chrome to brushed metal to vintage-style cut glass. Go to specialty hardware stores and browse for a look you love. These alone can pull your kitchen right out of the dark ages.

Upgrade Your Sink

Installing a new faucet, or even a new sink, can be a quick job for a plumber or handyperson. Make sure to measure carefully before you buy. You want your new sink to fit into the existing counter space. Take a digital picture of the existing sink with you to the hardware store, to help you remember details like the placement of the faucet and knobs.

A basic white Corian counter brightens a kitchen and is the perfect neutral especially when paired with these colorful canisters, which provide bold accents.

A few vivid orange accessories add energy to a kitchen defined by white paint and warm tones.

Upgrade Your Appliances

This means spending a bit of money, but replacing appliances can be quick and has a huge payoff in the look of the kitchen. If your refrigerator and dishwasher are old, chances are you'll also reap dividends in energy savings. If you can't buy new appliances, you can give the ones you have a new look with appliance-grade paint. Look for this at hardware or paint-supply stores.

Swap Out Your Countertop

Counters have almost as much impact as cabinets in the kitchen. If yours is in bad shape, think about replacing it. It's possible to do this fast if you go with in-stock solutions. Look at home improvement stores for options. I especially like marble, Corian®, Caesar-stone (a type of quartz countertop material), and even concrete. You'll definitely want to hire a pro for the installation.

The vivid grid of the backsplash is perfectly offset by an ad hoc arrangement of round ceramic containers.

A long-necked farmhouse-style faucet gives this sink a charming, look.

A new floor can be a weekend project. Here, homeowners painted a diamond pattern over a tired wood floor to give it new life.

A NEW FLOOR

It's time to take notice of the floor, because it can really make a dramatic difference in the look of your room! And you can make plenty of quick changes for big impact. Unlike laying down a simple rug, many of these ideas take commitment, so take the time to consider your options before you begin. Plan a week for this fix. I bet you'll love the results.

- **Install industrial rubber flooring.** Sold in rolls at home supply stores, this material is durable, comfortable underfoot, and available in colors like black, red, and white. The look is fresh and modern. It's easy to clean and what's more, that glass that falls on the floor is less likely to shatter.

- **Buy flooring tiles.** Sold under brand names like FLOR, these tiles are easy to install and remove. They come in a huge variety of colors and styles.

Super-strong industrial versions are available, which is a good idea for a high-traffic kitchen. You can use them to cover the whole floor or just to make a runner down the center if you have a galley-style space.

- **Paint your floor.** If your tile is in good shape but you don't like its color, paint it. Go to a paint store for industrial paint, which is durable enough to walk on, and apply several coats.

- **Go with epoxy.** You'll need a professional to install this polymer floor coating. Poured on right over the tile, it makes a smooth, seamless, and indestructible floor surface. The look is similar to a rubber floor, and it's even more practical. I love the look, but make sure you do, too, before trying this, because there's no fast removal method.

- **Install laminate flooring.** Floorboards made by Pergo® and similar companies are a snap to install and can go right over your existing flooring. You may want to hire a repair person for this project unless you're really skilled, because the saddle (the baseboard at the doorway) will probably need adjusting to the new floor level.

- **If you're really skilled and ambitious, tear the floor out.** You can sandblast and paint or refinish the subfloor beneath.

- **Home improvement wiz?** Install hardwood. In a small room like the kitchen, you can finish this project in about a week. And the effect is incomparable. But again, this is a project for those with advanced skills.

Replace Your Flooring

Look underfoot. Are you unhappy with your floor? Tearing out floor tiles and retiling really goes beyond the scope of speed decorating. But that doesn't mean you have to be stuck. Buying an area rug or runner in a bold color is the fastest solution. If you have a week's time and some handy helpers, you can also make a more dramatic change using one of the many quick flooring products on the market today. (See "A New Floor," above, for details.)

A COMFORTABLE ARRANGEMENT

Your kitchen is sparkling clean and undeniably stylish. But does it really work? The foundation of any kitchen consists of the stove, oven, refrigerator, dishwasher, sink, and workspace. If you have an eat-in kitchen, it also includes a table or counter and chairs or barstools. All of these elements must be well placed, well designed, and in good condition if they are to work for you and if you want anyone who joins you in the kitchen to be comfortable.

Chances are all the basic appliances are where they should be. Occasionally, though, you need to do a little tweaking in their placement. Often, the seating in the room needs rethinking. I once worked with a client, Stephanie, who had a beautiful, updated kitchen. At her breakfast bar, though, she'd been using regular dining chairs where stools should have gone. This arrangement made even simple meals difficult.

She wanted seats that would work for kids as well as adults and stand up to the rigors of her household. But she also wanted something a little bit plush.

Mixing seating styles can be the easiest way to accommodate a group. Here, a farm table pulls up to a long bench, while painted Windsor chairs flank the other three sides.

We found some online and had them delivered in just days. She chose stools with backs for extra comfort, upholstered in faux suede, which is an unbeatable fabric for kids. Even spilled soy sauce just beads up and rolls off. Once you identify the trouble spots, making your room comfortable is just a quick fix or two away.

Check Your Seating

Replace or repair chairs or stools that are damaged or don't fit the space. A great benefit to buying barstools is that they're super easy to shop for online. It's such a basic seat that you don't need to sit in a bunch and try them all out. Browse until you find a style you like, then buy and have them delivered. It's a huge time-saver.

Freshen Upholstery

If you're blessed with a breakfast nook, my favorite type of eating area, make sure the seat cushions are in good shape. If they're worn in spots, buy new ones, or choose upholstery fabric in colors you love and have them made.

Barstools are a fun and versatile seating option. Style choices abound. Iron stools are spare and practical in a modern space, and vinyl topped models with shiny chrome legs offer old-fashioned, diner appeal for a classic look. Backless, wooden-seated stools are fresh in an updated country kitchen.

Vivid color choices can really amp up your kitchen. Here, eye-opening sunflowers are balanced by matching dishware and lighting.

Go for a Whole New Look

Buying a new table and set of chairs is a fast way to update a kitchen, especially if you've been sitting and eating on hand-me-downs for years. But if your budget is tight, you can still get the feeling of a new set with of a few coats of paint. A basic table and chair set can take on a stylish new life if you brighten it with a paint color you love.

Rearrange Your Workspace

Your own comfort in the kitchen might be more about standing and cooking than sitting. Look at the arrangement and see if there is room for improvement. Is it easy to move from counter to stove to refrigerator? One thing I notice in some kitchens I visit is that the hinges on the refrigerator door are on the wrong side. The door opens away from the work area, making access awkward, and meaning extra steps for you.

Fixing this is fast. All you need is a strong helper and a screwdriver to take the hinges off and relocate them to the opposite side. Also, think about the placement of items you regularly use while you cook. Are your knives and chopping boards easy to reach but out of the way? I like to store knives in a drawer, right beneath the counter where I prep food.

NATURAL KITCHEN DECOR

Got a few hours to brighten up your kitchen? There's nothing nicer, or faster, than a bit of natural decoration to give your kitchen a personal, welcoming touch. I especially love edible bouquets and arrangements in the kitchen. What could be more appropriate?

- **BERRY BOUQUETS:** If you have blueberries, raspberries, wine berries, or blackberries near your home, this is bound to be a hit. Simply cut five to seven branches loaded with berries and arrange them in a large cylindrical vase filled halfway with water. Place it on the table, and you have an amazing centerpiece that's ready for snacking. We have blueberries in our yard, and my friends are always excited when I bring over a blueberry arrangement.

- **WHEATGRASS FLATS:** For a simple display, place wooden trays planted with wheatgrass on your table, counter, or windowsill. You can find wheatgrass at many flower markets, or order it online and have it delivered.

- **FARM STAND BOUQUET:** During the summer months, fresh herbs are abundant at farm stands and maybe in your own garden. I love to fill canning jars of various sizes with herbs such as dill, basil, and mint. Blue and green jars look especially good, and the herbs are handy when you want to make a quick salad.

LIGHT TO LIVE BY

Too often, people overlook lighting. The fact is, even if everything else is working in a kitchen, the right lighting will make it look better. It will also make it easier to do your work. Fortunately, lighting problems are easy to fix.

Replacing light fixtures was one of the first suggestions I made to my clients, the Stein's, when they moved into their new home. The kitchen had fluorescent fixtures that cast a gloomy, yellow glow. In order to create an inviting kitchen they swapped those lights for pendant schoolhouse fixtures. The result was fresh and clean.

Task lighting is just as important as ambient light, especially in a room designed for daily cooking chores. So it's important to consider both levels of light when looking for ways to brighten the room.

Replace an Uninspired Overhead Fixture

The fact is no one looks good in fluorescent light. And a boring, brassy hardware store ceiling light isn't much better. If your kitchen is equipped with one of these, make it a priority to replace it. A classic pendant light is a great choice; it will work in a kitchen of almost any style and offers practical yet flattering light.

●●● LET THE SUN SHINE IN

Adding or upgrading window treatments is something you can do in just a couple days, including shopping, if you buy off-the-rack styles. If your kitchen gets great natural light, make the most of it. If you also have a terrific view, you might even leave window treatments off altogether.

For added privacy, go with curtains in a sheer fabric, such as cotton voile. This is a good choice for a kitchen because it can easily be thrown into the washer when soiled. I also like roller-style solar shades. They're available in different opacities, so you can decide how much light filtering you want. And they open completely, to let in all that sun when you want it.

These sleek pendant lights, hanging between skylights, fit the modern aesthetic of this kitchen and provide appealing, ambient light.

Task lights are easy to mount under cabinets, and cast a glow exactly where you need it most.

Shed Some Light on Your Counters

If you don't have any under-cabinet task lights, add some. You can do this in a single day if you choose fixtures that don't require hard wiring. Look for "sticky lights." These small, battery-powered spotlights are held in place by adhesive and are a versatile option. Tuck them under cabinets if there is a lip to hide the fixture, and then just press each one to turn it on. If you have a little more time to drill and run cords to nearby outlets, install a few small, wired spotlights. These can connect to the same power source, so you can turn them all off or on at once.

Add a Little Glow

I love rope lighting, and it's a perfect way to give the kitchen a little added ambience. Just run it along the tops of your kitchen cabinets. To plug it in, run an extension cord down one side of a cabinet in an inconspicuous spot to the nearest outlet.

4. A Dining Room with Style

The dining room is prime entertaining space. It stands apart from other rooms that serve many functions, because it exists mainly for gathering and having fun. Think about lingering over great meals, socializing, and making use of your best dishes, candlesticks, and serving pieces. Now that's a beautiful thing!

Of course, not every house has a dedicated room for formal dining. But for those that do, this is a huge bonus. Even if you rarely have guests, the dining room serves a vital purpose. At its most basic, it's all about sitting and eating. It's where you spend quality time face-to-face with your family and treat them to meals that are more momentous than the rushed weekday breakfast. This is a more intimate kind of entertaining and equally important. The irony is homeowners who have this space often feel intimidated by its very formality. This can lead to neglect: You dress up the room then let it gather dust.

If you have a dining room, embrace your good luck by using it! Gather at the table for card games, or spread out and work on giant art projects. And, most important, eat there. Relegating the room to the category of "special"—used only on major holidays and for the occasional dinner party—means you're missing out. It's much more fun to make every day an event.

And it goes without saying that if you're planning to sell your home, a dining room that feels inviting and festive is a tremendous asset. When a potential buyer walks in, you want her immediately to imagine throwing a fabulous dinner party there.

What's your style? These high-backed wicker chairs may not be your grandmother's idea of a dining set, but they're right at home in this colorful, mid century–style room.

There are many ways to give your dining room this welcoming appeal. In my home, my husband and I use our china every day. We keep a candelabra on the table for instant glamour. It's fun and beautiful and makes even a quiet Monday night dinner a special occasion. As a bonus, it helps keep the passion alive, even after years of marriage!

Our habit of enjoying special meals in the dining room also makes it easy to have friends over for an impromptu dinner. We simply add a few more place settings at the table, and we're all ready.

Getting into a routine of luxurious meals in the dining room makes a lot of sense for the speed decorator. When you do so, you become much more invested in making the space as accommodating and stylish as possible. Likewise, if you actually pull out that good wedding china and your grandmother's silver, you'll constantly discover new, creative, beautiful ways to use them.

Ultimately, you'll save time, too. If company is coming for dinner or a real estate broker is on her way to snap some photos, you'll have everything you need and be ready to go. You've planned your centerpieces. Your silver has been often used and washed, so it doesn't need polishing. And you've mastered the art of setting a gorgeous table without the fuss of a tablecloth.

Of course, a welcoming dining room is about more than a well-set, and well-loved, table. As in any other room, it's important to think about comfortable, well-placed furniture, good lighting, and effective use of color. The dining room presents plenty of opportunities to let your personal style shine. If your dining room is rarely in use or feels too fussy and frozen in time, I have some quick and easy answers for you.

Here are the issues I most often encounter in dining rooms:

- The furniture is style challenged, or just plain uncomfortable. If it's too formal, it can feel like you're visiting Windsor Palace—too much pomp! You need to infuse it with fun.

- The room is dark. Dining room lighting should be cheerful and intimate, not clinical or so dim you can't see the food on your plate.

continued on p. 109

I love to set our dining table with china and crystal, silver taper candles in a black porcelain candelabra, and gorgeous arrangements of flowers and branches.

Every detail in its place. In this dining room, the sparkling, crystal-clear windows make a fantastic impression along with the carefully set table and sideboard.

- The room feels blah or jumbled together. Colors are bland, and the accessories create a feeling of chaos rather than defined style.

The first step in overcoming these hurdles is simply to start using the room. So that is your first assignment. Schedule a meal in the dining room and really experience it.

I know that changing habits can be tough, though, and don't worry—I won't leave you sitting in a too-hard chair, gazing over that chintz tablecloth and wondering what to do next. I'll walk you through taking stock of the situation, and then give you some great, fast fixes.

Just as with every other room, you don't need to do a complete overhaul to make a dramatic difference in your dining room. If you've been frozen by worries about the expense of renovating, or even investing in a new dining set, I can help. We won't be taking walls down to expand a cramped eating space or ripping up wall-to-wall carpet and installing hardwood, as jobs like that go beyond speed decorating. And while buying all new furniture is certainly an option, I have plenty of solutions that are easier on the wallet and just as fast. Put a few of my ideas to work, and you will almost feel like you have a whole new room—one that you'll love spending time in.

PUTTING EVERYTHING ON THE TABLE

As with every other room in the house, finding speed decorating fixes for the dining room starts with stepping back and evaluating the situation. Go back and review the three-step process I outlined in the Introduction, on page 20. Sit down at your table and really think it through. Take the time to go through the "Speed Decorating Question-naire," on page 19, and then look carefully at your answers.

How do you feel about the chair you're sitting in? Does the furniture itself need an update? Does the color scheme

Let go of the notion that everything must be formal and expensive in a well-decorated dining room. Here, an old door is beautifully repurposed as a long dining table.

●●● FIVE MUSTS FOR ANY DINING ROOM

1. **A chandelier.** Hanging a lavish fixture is the perfect way to add glamour to a dining room. This can be a pricey addition, but it doesn't have to be. Look at flea markets for older lights that simply need rewiring. Or find out when showrooms are getting rid of their samples for a bargain. My friend Barry picked up a gorgeous designer chandelier, which retailed for $1,500, for under $200 at a showroom that was discounting the style. Score!

2. **Stylish, comfortable chairs.** Repair wobbly legs or torn upholstery. This is quick and it won't cost much. If your chairs need complete reupholstering, there are beautiful fabrics at just about every price point, so look around for one that fits your budget. It's also important to relocate delicate antiques that might intimidate larger guests. Buying all new chairs can be a significant investment, but this is a worthwhile place to spend. Comfortable seating is a must for an inviting dining room.

3. **A table that fits.** It should be big enough for most dinner parties with plenty of room for chairs to fit comfortably around the table.

4. **Candles.** Have fresh tapers on hand, and trim those wicks so they burn with a clean, clear flame.

5. **Fresh flowers.** They brighten any space.

of the room? Look around at the walls and up at the ceiling. You might find that changes as minor as picking up a few new accessories and installing a dimmer switch will make all the difference.

Sometimes identifying the trouble spots gets tricky, because you're emotionally attached to the furniture you have. I saw this when working with newlyweds Valerie and Tom. They had moved into a new home and inherited their parents' furniture. Valerie asked for help because they also had all kinds of new accessories they'd received as wedding gifts, and the style clashed with the hand-me-downs. I knew we needed a plan that would allow them to entertain in a style that reflected who they were.

During the evaluation, it became clear that all the furniture had to go. The American Colonial and Queen Anne–style pieces felt too formal for Valerie's unfussy, laid-back style, not to mention their modern, open living space. They needed a new look. We made a shopping list of dining room chairs, a buffet for storage, a new chandelier, and a round table instead of the old rectangular one (much better for socializing!).

We were able to find showroom samples available for purchase right off the floor, so we had an instant transformation. We painted the walls a creamy café au lait color to create a distinct dining area. The color palette, ebony wood mixed with soft creamy champagne colors and ivory velvet, created an airy, festive vibe.

I think you'll find, as Valerie and Tom did, that once you can clearly articulate the challenges you're facing, the solutions are a snap.

I'm going to assume here that you've already given this room a good, thorough cleaning. Unlike busier spaces like the kitchen, the dining room is less likely to be

A space made for celebrating. In the dining room of our apartment, an elegant yet fun table setting, comfy modern armchairs, great light, and a gorgeous view make every dinner feel like a special occasion.

Adding a new piece of furniture in a bold hue can make a dramatic difference in a dining room, fast. This orange sideboard is not only practical; its sleek style and eye-popping color bring the room to life.

plagued by piles of paper and other clutter. But if you're looking up at dirty sconces, windows clouded by fingerprints, and you can write your name in the dust on the sideboard, you know you have work to do. A sparkling clean room looks fantastic.

Dinner Is Served

When I work with a client, this is always one of my very first questions: How much time do you have? The answer is crucial and determines how much decorating we can accomplish.

Is your deadline tonight? You can do a lot in one day in the dining room. Give the room a deep cleaning, pull out your best accessories and spruce them up, and bring in some more for added flair. You can also change the bulbs in your light fixtures and use candles to create terrific ambience.

In a long weekend, you can really have fun with color. Change all your table linens; even paint the walls. A full week gives you time to shop for furniture or to overhaul the pieces you have with a new stain or fresh coat of paint. You can also have an electrician come and wire for new lighting and install a spectacular fixture that changes the mood of the room.

If you don't have a deadline already, set one. As we discussed in the kitchen chapter (see page 84), this is a great excuse to throw a party. Invite friends to see your new dining room. Then make it happen!

(see page 84)

MAGIC-WAND MAKEOVER

PUT YOUR SIDEBOARD TO WORK

If you have a sideboard, buffet, or even a bar cart in your dining room, that can be a decorative element, too. Make the most of it for your next party.

- **"DECORATE" WITH WINE AND COCKTAIL ACCOUTREMENTS:** Set out glasses, mixers, and liquors and let your guests make their own drinks. Have a cheese plate and olives set out. Or keep it simple and line up flutes to serve champagne when guests arrive. My husband is a wine professional (see whatwouldmikeydrink.com) so it's always champagne to kick off the evening in our home. We'll offer caviar, too. That's my favorite! Another luxurious way to set the mood is with foie gras and a sauterne.

- **SET UP THE BUFFET FOR A PARTY THEME:** A Thanksgiving dinner, a spring brunch, a pool party . . . whatever strikes your fancy. Shop for kitschy, inexpensive serving pieces that fit your theme and its corresponding color scheme. Arrange them so their heights are staggered. This will add a quick, fun focal point to the room!

With dining chairs, put comfort first. Guests happily sink into these plump wing chairs, and when the table isn't in use, pull them into another room for conversation or movie viewing.

DINING ROOM FURNITURE FUNDAMENTALS

In the dining room, the most essential pieces of furniture are the table and chairs. There may be sideboards and hutches to consider, but they are secondary. It's vital to have chairs that feel as good as they look. The table should be graciously proportioned and appropriate to the scale of the room. And, of course, its style should appeal to you.

A Good Chair

Having good, comfy dining room seating should be a primary goal. Don't hold on to chairs you don't like. I once worked with a client who had moved from a hundred-year-old brownstone to a modern, downtown loft. She had a set of upholstered, chintz-patterned chairs that just didn't work in the hip new space. She was quickly growing to hate those chairs.

She could have thrown them out and gotten a new set, but since the pieces were essentially well made, I suggested she lacquer them white and reupholster them in a white pony skin for a fresh new look. It was a big leap, but it really worked in her space.

If you hate the chairs you're sitting on, get rid of them now and get something new. It's better to sit on cushions on the floor than to squirm awkwardly on the wrong chairs.

Go out and find something you love and dive in. Buy at least four—six is even better. If the dining table, without its extension, only seats four comfortably then position

There's no rule that says all your seating has to match. Here, an upholstered bench and a couple of chairs create a cozy, attractive dining spot.

any extras in another room. Spare armchairs can go in the living room for extra seating, or you can tuck them away in a bedroom. When guests come over, put in the table extension and round up the chairs.

When shopping for chairs, use your imagination. Try upholstered wingbacks, for instance. They're super comfortable and great for playing games around the table as well as for eating. Or maybe forgo the standard furniture stores and visit antiques shops. A set of mismatched chairs can be quirky and fun. If they're sturdy and you like their shapes but their finishes are on the shabby side, you can lacquer them all black or white for a cool, unified look.

Alternatively, if you like the shape of your chairs but they're in need of maintenance, this is the time to get that work done. Maybe you've sidelined a couple chairs that need repair, and you're getting by with subbing in kitchen seating when company comes. Go ahead and take those to a pro for fixing. An update like this is a lot easier than finding all new chairs, because you don't have to choose a new style. It can be quite inexpensive, too, depending on the work you need done. It's a smart option to explore. And having that full set again will feel almost as good as getting something new.

The Right Table

The most important thing about a dining room table is that it must fit your space. That means choosing the table carefully, but it can also mean thinking creatively about the space itself.

I once worked with a client who had her heart set on a round dining table large enough to seat eight. She was newly married and wanted enough space to have dinner parties for her friends and extended family and for hosting her husband's occasional work dinners. But her cozy dining room was too small for such a table, so instead, we relocated the dining area, designating a spacious nook off the living room for dining. This transformed the dining room itself into more of a study and was a spectacular way to redefine the

DINING TABLE MAKEOVER

If you have a long weekend, you have time enough to paint a dining table and a set of chairs. Here are some things to keep in mind when working:

- **Work in a well-ventilated area.**

- **Clean the items before beginning.** Use fine sandpaper to smooth any bumps or marks, then wipe down with a damp cloth to remove all traces of dust.

- **Choose the right products.** A white, high-gloss paint will create an attractive, durable finish. If in doubt about which paint to buy, ask at the paint store for the best finish for your table. Follow the manufacturer's directions for application, and be sure to prime first! A salesperson at the paint store can also direct you to a primer that suits the surface.

- **If you're using a color** other than a standard white or black, try lacquering a "test board" first to be sure you like your color choice.

A chandelier not only illuminates the meal but also helps to establish the style of the room. Here, a red-and-green-painted fixture adds a funky counterpoint to a vintage dining table.

function of the room while allowing my client to have everything she wanted—all without tearing down walls.

Then we bought a dramatic round table with leaves to expand for guests. We placed four of the chairs around the table for everyday use and housed four in other rooms. There was no electric box above the new dining table, so we bought a chandelier that didn't require hardwiring. We had a hook installed above the table in the ceiling and ran the cord down the wall in a corner. It was perfect.

Replacing a dining table and chair set or even creating a new dining space can be wonderful. But there are ways to add pizzazz to what you already own. My husband and I have a dining set given to us by my in-laws. And while the pieces are good quality, they're in a French country style that's not me. My solution? A coat of paint. A bright white lacquer erases many fussy details and creates a cleaner, more modern look.

Be bold when it comes to making changes. If you don't like your furniture, after all, you have little to lose. Take a chance on a fun color—white, black, or even pink. Go for it.

LIGHT THAT'S INVITING

The right furniture makes a dining room comfortable and stylish, but good lighting really sets the mood. The dining room is more dramatic when all the lighting is concentrated on the table, leaving the rest of the room a little bit shadowy. This draws people closer together and has the effect of warming the space.

The Chandelier

A chandelier is the focal point of the dining room. Hung over the dining room table it adds height, drama, and ambience. It creates instant style.

There is a tremendous variety of chandeliers available in lighting stores, and you should feel free to choose one you love. As a general guideline, if your ceiling is high, you can go for a dramatic, multi-tiered crystal chandelier. If the ceiling is a

This brass fixture, designed in 1950 by Mathieu Mategot, offers a more modern twist on the chande-lier. Hung high like a ceiling fixture, it casts a warm glow and lends a feeling of spaciousness to the low-ceilinged room.

This vintage chande-lier is made of painted wood and has an organic appeal.

MAGIC-WAND
MAKEOVER

CREATE A CANDLE DISPLAY

If you've been pulling out the same two candlesticks for every dinner party for the past several years, it's time to mix it up. What a couple of candles do well, numerous candles do better. To add drama but keep the look elegant, stick to an uncomplicated color scheme.

In a quick shopping trip, you can pick up a variety of candles and holders with a common theme. Stagger clear crystal candleholders in different shapes and sizes to create a festive table. White holders with white candles look great, as does an assortment of smoked crystal or black porcelain mixed with white candle tapers for a bold black-and-white theme. Keep it simple and you'll add texture and dimension without creating visual pandemonium.

standard 9-ft. height (or lower), then stick to a simpler fixture, such as one with a drum shade, or a single-tier chandelier. Hang the light about 2 ft. above the table for the best effect.

Sconces

Sconces, which cast a soft glow along the periphery of the room, are another nice option for a dining room. For the quickest, easiest installation, you can simply run their cords down the wall, and disguise them with wire molding (available in hardware stores). Paint the molding to match the wall color and it will disappear.

Candlelight

Electric lights can work wonders, but the most low-tech way to accomplish a warm, intimate effect is to turn down the lights and burn some candles.

Be sure to use enough to shed a gracious amount of light on the table. My husband likes a romantic dinner, but he also likes to be able to see his food. So I tend to mix it up with lots of clear glass candleholders of various heights and styles. The glow is soft but vibrant and creates an enchanting vibe.

You can use a variety of candlesticks, candelabras, and votive holders to create height and drama on the table.

A Dimmer Switch

To ensure that electric light offers a soft complement to the glimmer of your candles, have dimmer switches installed. This is another quick task for an electrician, and it costs almost nothing. If you're throwing a dinner party, you can bring the lights down for a quieter mood and then turn them up for the poker tournament that follows.

A bouquet of pink peonies, arranged in a clear glass vase filled with limes, is fresh and bold.

STYLE MATTERS

Okay, so you have a great table and chairs, and your lighting is right. But maybe the room still doesn't feel like "you." This is where the fun comes in. I love adding elements of style through clever use of color, well-chosen accessories, and imaginative tabletop displays.

Pick your favorite vase and keep it filled with flowers. Replace them every week. Hang artwork that inspires you. It doesn't have to be an expensive painting. In fact, your own photographs might mean a whole lot more to you. I have a client, for instance, who has been married for at least nine years.

She and her husband met in college; she was from Boston, he was from down south. They had a terrific collection of photos from their years together. I suggested she pick nine photos, one for each of those years. We printed them out in black and white and framed them in a grid to create a "love wall." This dramatic personal touch added loads of visual interest to the room.

A table setting defined by brilliant sunset colors gives a tabletop instant glamour.

●●● START YOUR OWN ART "GALLERY"

Hanging artwork is an incomparable way to add style and personality to any room, and the dining room in particular makes a terrific backdrop. You can't build an entire collection in a week, but this is enough time to seek out one great piece and hang it. That will inspire you to keep going.

Choose art that makes you feel happy or even spurs the appetite. The dining room of my friend Karen Boltax, a gallery owner, is a great example. The room has one long, horizontal photo—depicting a glowing fire—against the wall. It creates a cozy, warm vibe.

I recommend collecting art that you love. It doesn't have to be fancy or expensive; one of my favorite art pieces is a set of silver antlers I bought on impulse and hung on the wall of my dining room for kitschy appeal.

I also love displaying paintings that are meaningful to me. The painting on my dining room wall came from Rod Massey, an artist in Minnesota, my home state. Start seeking out artists and supporting them. Begin with just one piece. Hang it simply, at eye level or a bit lower. Remember that people spend a long time in the

dining room, so you don't want art as high as you might hang it in a hallway, for instance. Over time, you'll have a valuable collection of pieces.

Color

Sedate hues have their place, but a pop of bold color can really make a dining room come alive.

One of my favorite dining rooms belongs to friends Mimi and Steve. The room, including dining chairs upholstered in vibrant orange faux suede, came from my friend Fred's store, Home 114. He furnished their whole home in a modern style. The color really shines against the otherwise quiet wood tones in the room and gives visitors an immediate impression: dinner is always juicy and fun.

If you prefer a muted color palette, you can introduce color in small dramatic ways. Cluster a group of bright-colored vases on the table or sideboard. Or invest in a cheerful area rug. This will provide color and pattern but can also help to define the dining space.

CREATE SEASONAL CENTERPIECES

Boring centerpieces need not apply! You can whip up a lively display that celebrates the time of year in as little as a few minutes.

- **SPRING:** Set out an arrangement of potted tulips or other bulbs.

- **SUMMER:** Try something beachy, such as hurricanes filled with seashells and starfish or canning jars with votives nestled in sand.

- **FALL:** Warm the mood with a vast cluster of candles or a grand candelabra.

- **WINTER:** Set out a bunch of paper whites or a huge, triple-stem white orchid.

Tablescapes

I love getting creative with tabletop decorations. There are endless possibilities that go beyond the usual flower arrangements and folded napkins. I like to mix and match china patterns for a fun, less-fancy mood. I often forgo a linen tablecloth entirely, choosing instead to use placemats, table runners, or just great place settings on their own. This saves time and looks fresh and modern.

Centerpieces can be imaginative and are especially fun if you change them with the seasons. (See "Create Seasonal Centerpieces," above, for ideas.) Or think about the mood that you're trying to set with the meal. Is it a romantic dinner for two? A raucous holiday party? It's fun, fast, and inexpensive to choose a theme and "prop" the table to coordinate.

Also, remember "seasonal" means not having to pay extra for the super-fancy imported bouquets. This is speed decorating, so it should be easy on your budget and on your brain. Some of the best centerpiece materials abound right at the farmer's market or even a roadside stand. You'll notice throughout this book that I've focused on blooms that are not overly showy but simply delightful—and local.

A piece of coral anchoring a stack of napkins and a bunch of hydrangeas freshly cut from the yard add vivid color to a casual table setting.

"THERE IS NO TIME FOR CUT-AND-DRIED MONOTONY."

—COCO CHANEL

5. The Luxurious Bedroom

The bedroom is your most personal space; so when I work with clients, I always focus on creating a soothing, rest-inducing atmosphere in this room. Decadent decorating here is its own reward. Though your guests may rarely see inside, when you create an amazing retreat, you'll find yourself wanting to show it off.

There are occasions, of course, when outsiders will see your bedroom. If you're having overnight guests, chances are good someone will wander in. And if you're selling and planning an open house, you can count on potential buyers inspecting the room's every nook and cranny. The goal is to help them see the room as if it were their own. It needs to be stylish and inspiring so that they can imagine curling up and getting comfortable.

Speaking of overnight guests, don't forget to devote some effort to your guest room, too. Take the time to make it feel like an inviting haven. Your friends and family will thank you.

Most people think it's more important to splurge on a public space such as the dining or living rooms, but the bedroom is the place to treat yourself (and your loved ones) like royalty. Decorate for pleasure. That means getting rid of outdated features and layering on the luxury.

I saw this work firsthand with my clients Sara and Doug, who have been married over ten years and felt drained every time they went into the bedroom. They both worked at home, and Doug had turned the walk-in closet into a home office. The first time we met, they complained about the wall color and said the room felt claustrophobic, but they didn't know why.

A fresh color scheme brightens a bedroom. In this sweet, airy room, a vintage coverlet and vases of blooms on the desk complement rose-colored walls.

A petite, crystal chandelier is a romantic lighting choice over the bed.

Looking around the room, I could see the problems right away. The sconces by the bed were a dreary black and their style didn't match the Zen feeling of the room's other furniture. On the bed, there were black sheets that were faded to a threadbare charcoal and looked about twenty years old. A couple of decades ago, this room may have had some magic, but now it looked as if the love was gone.

To bring it up to date and add some magic, I suggested they purchase crisp linens, throw in a fuzzy rug, and swap the sconces with elegant polished nickel fixtures. I also coaxed them to relocate the office.

We painted the walls a warm gray; the soothing tone reflected and enhanced the room's natural light. Overall, the result was a room that looked like it was loved. And its owners had a brand new outlook. (And love life!)

OTHER BEDROOMS IN THE HOUSE

Of course, some bedrooms are inherently more "public." Guest rooms deserve special consideration and require a few extra touches to provide the comforts of home for your visitors.

Kids' rooms, too, tend to get a lot of traffic. It's often the play space of choice when friends visit, and lively touches are especially fun to show off. There should be plenty of room to store toys, and the room should be cheerful and colorful enough to inspire imagination and dreams.

In any sort of bedroom, the space works best when dedicated to its primary functions. If possible, keep paperwork in the home office, or at least out of sight. Relegate exercise equipment to the gym. And scale back on huge televisions and other electronic equipment.

The bedroom is the place to spoil yourself. In our bedroom, we've layered Italian linens over a handmade organic cotton bed from Sweden. A gold lamp, gray velvet empire curtains (made and installed by my in-laws, Linda and Morty), and artwork from our friend Tracy complete the lavish theme.

129

My favorite bedroom is one that is well organized. It should feel calm and have abundant clean, clear spaces and layers of soft textures.

Here are the decorating challenges I most often encounter in bedrooms:

- There's too much going on. Clutter, either physical or visual, via busy patterns and raucous colors, detract from the atmosphere.

- The space feels too small or cramped.

- It's cold and impersonal. More comfortable furniture and better accessories are necessary to create a cozy, interesting vibe.

- The lighting doesn't fit the mood of the room.

If you have any or all of these issues in your bedrooms, I have ideas that will help you make big changes fast. In almost every case, you can do the work yourself. You might want to call an electrician to put in a new light fixture, but you won't be talking to contractors about building an addition for that roomy walk-in closet. We'll find ways to use the space you have now to its best advantage and create an inviting, peaceful haven.

An armchair in a corner provides a shot of color and is perfect for curling up with a book or strapping on stilettos.

For a peaceful space, keep visual clutter to a minimum. Here, an all-white bed is at the center of a pared-down bedroom; a large red painting and a plush rug infuse this space with passion and personality.

THE HEART OF THE PROBLEM

You spend every morning and evening in your bedroom, so you're probably more familiar with it than any other room. To analyze what works and what doesn't in the space, take a step back and try to look at it as if you're seeing it for the first time. Remember, the first step in speed decorating is always evaluating the situation: Figure out if the room meets your needs and makes you happy. Then you'll know what you need to fix.

When my clients, Cathy and Rob, told me they felt cramped in their master bedroom, they couldn't explain why. The room was spacious, after all. I understood the problem. They had lived in their sprawling apartment for twenty-one years. Their youngest son had just graduated from college, and they were ready to downsize into a new, smaller space. They were so used to looking at the bookcases overflowing with dated paraphernalia that lined the walls, the off-center bed, and even the broken lamp in the corner, that they hardly noticed those details anymore. It was clearly time to move on.

●●● FAST, FUN TOUCHES FOR KIDS' ROOMS

While your own bedroom might be the picture of serenity, kids' rooms should stimulate the imagination. Sure, you want them to be conducive to rest, too (room darkening shades can be a bonus here), but this is a creative space. Feel free to go a little wild.

- **Add color:** Bold colors add visual punch to the bedroom. For instance, I love rich blues on the walls, or in the sheets and accessories, with lime green accents. Try some rich, saturated jewel tones here and there for texture. One great place to find these is in Marimekko® bed linens. Fun and cheerful, these feature prints in organic shapes and brilliant splashes of color.

- **Define the space:** Since a child's room is more than a place for sleeping, it's best to have a designated area for each function. Think about ways to mark out spaces for play, homework, and romping around. You might set up a table for drawing, some storage bins for toys and supplies along a wall, and an area full of soft floor pillows for rough-and-tumble play.

In updating their bedroom, we began by removing clutter, giving away books, and rethinking the arrangement of sculptures and other items on the shelves. While everything was off the shelves, we had them thoroughly cleaned. This is one area often overlooked in cleaning, and dust builds up fast. We then arranged the books by color and size and the other items into a beautiful display around them.

We of course replaced the broken lamp, and removed everything from under the bed, too. Keeping that area completely open and clear of clutter helps to set a peaceful mood. The result was that the room felt sparkly clean and spacious, and everything had a place.

When doing your evaluation, examine all the surfaces in the room. Look at the floor and under the bed. (Can you even see under there?) Lie down on the bed and think about how you feel. If your guest room needs an update, think about the details that matter to you when you visit someone else's home.

Even a bedroom with minimal furnishings can be very comfortable. Here, a tray with a water carafe placed by the bed, along with a portrait and a modern floor lamp, does a beautiful job of standing in for a night table.

Set Your Alarm

How you address these issues will largely depend on how much time you have. Do you have houseguests arriving tomorrow? Next week? Or maybe your anniversary is in a few days and you'd like to spice up the bedroom to surprise your spouse.

In just a day, you can make great strides by eliminating clutter, buying all new bed linens, or adding accessories to unify the space. A long weekend will allow you to get more creative, swapping out light fixtures, trying new window treatments, or organizing your closets and other storage spaces.

When you pare down on clutter, tiny details have big impact. On this windowsill, a miniature painting and an espresso cup serving as a vase for a single daisy create a beautiful vignette.

If you have a full week, you have time for the big changes—go ahead and shop for new furniture or floor coverings and have them delivered, rethink your upholstery, maybe even update the color scheme.

Determine your deadline now and set your goals. The key to successful speed decorating is creating a game plan and sticking with it. All the hard work will pay off when you enjoy that sumptuous boudoir and drift into sweet dreams.

RECLAIM YOUR CALM

It's natural for a bedroom to get cluttered; we tend to fill our living spaces, no matter how big or small they are. But a room packed to the gills is not relaxing. When I walk into a bedroom, one of the first things I notice is whether there is too much "stuff." And I'm not immune to it myself. Sometimes when I'm working and traveling a lot, my own clothes accumulate on the closet floor, shoes get scattered, and the bed goes unmade.

So like anyone, I have to pay attention and be diligent about this on a regular basis. It's one thing if it's a few days of accumulation; it's another to let forty years worth of things build up.

Keep It Simple

One way to guarantee a good night's sleep is to keep work out of the bedroom. There's nothing sexy about bills or work problems. You'll enjoy your waking hours a whole lot more, too, if your bedroom is beautiful and peaceful, not a bustling extension of your office. So, *put the papers away.*

If you have a separate home office, keep your paperwork there. Designate a space far away from the bedroom to file papers and bills. If your only workspace is a corner of your bedroom, change it. This is like separation of church and state: It's time to divide your living and resting space. Even a pretty file box you keep in a kitchen cabinet is much better than bringing it into the bedroom.

Limit bedside items to a few of your favorite things. A vintage painting and a vase of flowers picked from the garden are at home next to the bed in this artful room.

Walkways are key in a bedroom that feels spacious. Here, a king-size bed takes center stage, but there is clear floor space on all sides, so the feeling is open, not cramped.

What should you have beside the bed? Only the basics. You need a good lamp for reading and a great book or two (or twelve, if reading is your passion, but stack them neatly!) And definitely a vase of fresh flowers. As for the table itself, it should be something you like. See "A New Nightstand," on page 148 for some of my favorite bedside table ideas.

Take the same approach with the top of the dresser and any other surfaces in the bedroom. They'll look better and the mood of the room will stay fresh and fun if you're careful to keep day-to-day clutter to a minimum.

The Closet and Beyond

If you want your bedroom to be a calming retreat, you simply can't have clothes strewn about. So get that wardrobe under control. You can box up and donate items you haven't worn in years, and move off-season things out of your bedroom and into storage. Follow my "Closet Makeover," at right, to get started. Or, if you find the task too overwhelming, call in an organizing specialist. But get the job done.

The Television

The most relaxing boudoirs are not equipped with televisions. But if you can't go to sleep at night without it, at least keep the set to a reasonable size or make sure it tucks away

---

CLOSET MAKEOVER

This exercise will help you create a closet you love, in just a three-day weekend. Plan to spend the first day or two doing the heavy work. Reserve day three for dropping off charity items, bringing items needing repair to the tailor, and shopping (the reward!).

1. **Begin by taking everything out of the closet.** Sort clothes, shoes, and accessories into three piles: Keep, Giveaway, and Repair.

2. **Vacuum the floor and scrub down the shelves.** If your closet is equipped with only a single rod and shelf, consider installing a closet system, available in home supply and organizing stores, to expand storage.

3. **Paint the interior a vibrant color** such as shocking pink or poppy red. This will energize you as you choose your clothes in the morning.

4. **Before you put any clothes back** into the closet, try on each item from the Keep piles in front of a mirror. Ask yourself, "Do I love this?" If the answer is no, then drop it in the Giveaway pile. If you love it, but it needs repair or hemming, put it in the Repair pile.

5. **Now that you have purged your closet,** get rid of those Giveaway items within 24 hours, before fear of replacement hits.

6. **Send the pants that need hemming** and shirts with missing buttons to the tailor. Shoes that need resoling should go to a cobbler now, too.

7. **Congratulations!** You have a closet filled with things you love. You should also have some empty space. So go shopping to treat yourself!

A few decadent decorative details can really make a bedroom feel good. Here, a nude painting above the bed is quietly seductive.

in an armoire or cabinet to maintain the peaceful mood. Those jumbo screens belong in the family or media room. (For more TV tips, see "A Living Room for all Occasions," on page 47.)

OPEN IT UP

When your bedroom is really clean and clutter-free, it will automatically feel more peaceful. But even a very clean room will still feel cramped if its proportions are small. I have some speedy ways to open up your space.

The Right Arrangement

Center the bed against a wall to make the room feel larger. Shoving the bed into the corner makes a room feel cramped and off balance; plus, it makes it difficult to make the bed. Even if left with a slim walkway on each side, a centered bed will be an improvement. Aim the foot of the bed away from the door, if possible, for better energy.

On the Walls

Artwork, artfully arranged, can do wonders for a space. In the bedroom, go for art that is tasteful but sets a relaxing or seductive mood. Black and white photography always looks good in the bedroom, too. You can do a grouping of small pieces or pick one big piece for over the bed. If you are using smaller pieces, group them in odd numbers for the best visual balance.

I like long horizontal pieces over the bed, because they make the room feel more expansive. The shape also mimics the sleeper's position, for a harmonious effect.

If you prefer paintings to photos, look for calming colors. Whatever you do, buy art that moves and inspires you. Support local artists and buy things you love. It doesn't have to be expensive—look to thrift stores or flea markets. Originality counts. You might even get creative and make your own artwork. Buy a canvas at the art store and paint something, or spend an afternoon seeking out photos that remind you of sleeping, seduction, or rest. Frame them in a group of three or enlarge one to hang over your bed.

Windows and Natural Light

Natural sunlight makes a room come alive, so I like to go for window treatments that frame the window and are a little bit lavish but still let in that sunshine. I

This bright, white bedroom gets tons of natural light from its tall window. Floor-to-ceiling, sheer curtains let the sun shine through while providing just enough privacy.

A well-lit bedroom will have a welcoming glow. Here, this table lamp suits the style of this playful guest room and provides cozy light for reading in bed.

find that soft, white sheers are often all that are needed to dress a window in the bedroom. They create a billowy, gossamer feeling and are especially dreamy in the summertime when soft breezes blow through them.

SET THE MOOD WITH LIGHTING

One of the most essential details in an inviting bedroom is great lighting. This became crystal clear in my last rental apartment. My husband and I loved the spacious room but detested the brass hardware-store light installed on the ceiling when we moved in. The fixture itself was uninspired, and the light it cast was harsh.

No matter what else I did with furniture or accessories, I knew the room wouldn't be finished until I replaced that light! So I quickly found a charming crystal chandelier and made the switch. The new fixture was elegant, and its soft light set just the right mood in the room.

Of course, revamping your entire bedroom lighting plan can be time-consuming. But plenty of fixes fit into a speed decorating makeover. It can take as little as a few hours to replace a graceless ceiling fixture with a pair of bedside lamps for a more romantic glow. Likewise, you can quickly hang a chandelier, as I did, for a boudoir with a bit of higher drama.

Bedroom lighting should be warm, flattering, and adjustable. This globe pendant light in amber glass casts a clear, soft light; it's on a dimmer to suit changing moods.

A simple, shaded chandelier is a sweet touch in a bedroom.

If you've already splurged on the best mattress you could find, or if you have your heart set on an indulgent set of Italian linens, you may be hesitant to invest in light fixtures, too. But remember that although there are plenty of pricey fixtures out there, budget-friendly ideas abound. In fact, some of my favorite fixes are practically free. Repurposing lamps from the attic or flea market, for instance, is fun, fast, and low-cost. So don't hesitate to go for the glow you want.

MAKE BAD LIGHT DISAPPEAR

If you have an overhead fixture that you really don't like but can't replace right away, you can make it "disappear." *Turn it off.* Get some lamps, either borrowed from other rooms in the house or on a quick shopping trip, and place them on bedside tables and on the dresser. Poof! That overhead light is magically gone.

Later, you can have an electrician come out and swap the light for a chandelier, a pendant light, or any other fixture that enhances the style of the room. Alternatively, you can have him remove the light and cap off the light box. After all, in the bedroom, sometimes the best light is no light at all.

Every Light in Its Place

In the bedroom, lighting needs are simple. There should be adequate task lighting—for reading in bed, for example, and for sizing up your wardrobe. And there should be light that helps to set a relaxing, romantic mood.

You can easily meet these needs with a light on either side of the bed and an attractive ceiling fixture. You might also place a floor lamp next to a comfy chair for putting on shoes or reading. A small lamp on top of a dresser is an optional touch that can make a stylish statement.

When looking for bedside and floor lamps, feel free to get creative. Look around the house, in your grandmother's attic, at tag sales, and so on for fun fixtures you can repurpose for the bedroom.

I generally like to keep light fixtures smaller and softer in the bedroom. One easy guideline for a nightstand lamp is that it should be about as long as your arm. This is not the place to add bulk.

Wall-mounted sconces are also a great option. They cast a soft light, but one that's focused enough for reading. Place one on either side of the bed, about a foot or two above the mattress, and run the cords down to the nearest wall outlets.

In every case, have a dimmer switch installed, too, so you can turn down those lights when only the barest glimmer will do. This is an inexpensive and fast fix. You can do it yourself if you're handy with wiring, or tack it onto a list of little projects and have an electrician come out and take care of them all at once.

Finally, don't forget the candles. Place them on nightstands, the dresser, the windowsill . . . and light them whenever you want to set a romantic scene.

Books stacked on a side chair make a sturdy base for a bedside lamp on this impromptu nightstand.

A Lucite™ lamp, filled with red coral and topped with a square shade, is a bright choice atop this heavy wood dresser.

Big, colorful pieces on the walls can make a room feel grand. Here, a large sailfish is on dramatic display over a dresser.

Color brings life to a bedroom. Luxuriant shades of green in this room—in curtains, fireplace tiles, artwork, and brilliantly painted walls—make a lush combination.

ADD A DASH OF COLOR

A clean, well-arranged, and well-lit bedroom will feel peaceful, but for a style all your own, nothing goes further, faster, than color. Maybe you've been living with tired walls that haven't been repainted in ages and linens and accessories that showcase last decade's style. Or perhaps you're afraid to experiment with color and are spending your nights in a world of white and beige. In any case, a burst of color can really revitalize your room.

Jade walls look crisp and calm when framed by clean white trim.

Aqua velvet and aquarium blue silk throw pillows lend both softness and vitality to this wooden rocker.

Quick Hits

Accessories, bedding, rugs, and window treatments are all easy opportunities for adding color. Layer on colorful textures: In a room with white walls, an electric blue throw and gossamer window treatments in a vibrant springtime green, for instance, will make you feel refreshed. Once you've selected a color scheme, a day's shopping trip can mean a delightful update for your bedroom.

A New Hue

One of the fastest and most effective ways to introduce color to any room is by painting the walls. You can pick just one wall for a brightening effect or redo the whole room. Pick a color that makes you feel happy.

I did this when we lived in our first apartment in New York City. Our bedroom got very little natural light, so I painted the room a brilliant orange to give it a jolt of color. It felt like the sunrise in the morning. The point is to pick something you love.

To open up your space and make your bedroom feel larger, try painting the walls and moldings all one color from floor to ceiling. This works well both in newer houses, with stark walls and uninteresting trim, and in classic, prewar homes. When I was in Sweden, I noticed they painted beautiful, old-style Gustavian buildings this way. I loved that it made the ceiling feel higher. Of course, if you prefer a more traditional look, you can't go wrong with a crisp, white frame of trim around a bold wall color.

GET COMFORTABLE

If your room is clean and well arranged, you've made a soothing start. Now it's time to add some indulgent touches. Things like linens, smaller furnishings, and a few well-placed accessories provide opportunities to inject your personality into the space.

A great example of this is the bedroom of my friend John. A bachelor, he is very creative and has excellent taste. He'd renovated his apartment a few years ago but hadn't gotten around to finishing. When I visited him, I saw that in spite of good-quality furniture and bedding, his bedroom felt dark and uninspiring. It was missing the personal touches that really made a statement.

We spiced things up by hanging white, gauzy window treatments (purchased off-the-rack), along with a set of white wood blinds. We bought a new wingback armchair for reading and installed sconces from Crate & Barrel above the bed. His bedroom was small, so we kept just one nightstand. We cleared it of bills and papers and added a vase of roses and a few books by John's favorite Beat poets. The bed was layered with a new cashmere throw for a comfy touch. Overall, the look was soft and inviting but masculine. It suited John perfectly.

Whether you're decorating your own room or a guest room, a few carefully chosen details can make all the difference.

Every detail counts. This stitched leather doorknob adds to a bedroom's luxe factor.

A Dream-Worthy Bed

Even if you don't spend a dime on the rest of your bedroom, you should invest in an amazing bed. We spend more time sleeping than doing anything else in life, so be as comfortable as possible. Assuming the mattress itself is in good shape, go ahead and splurge on finely woven, high-quality linens.

My husband and I treated ourselves to an all organic-cotton bed that was hand-made in Sweden. We covered it with a simple, warm yet airy duvet in white. Both were investments but really worth it.

MAGIC-WAND MAKEOVER   DRESS YOUR BED

In an afternoon's time, you can shop for a new wardrobe for your bed. There's no better or faster way to give the room an indulgent upgrade. Here are some tips:

- **QUALITY:** When you're shopping, focus on more than just thread count. The quality of the cotton itself is most important. Always look for Egyptian cotton, which has the longest staple of all cottons—meaning a smoother, finer, softer fabric. And seek out linens made in Italy if you can. Artisans in that country have centuries of expertise to draw upon when creating and finishing fabrics, and they are usually the very best. (See Resources, on page 196 for sellers of fine linens.)

- **PATTERN AND COLOR:** When buying bed linens, seek out muted colors if you want to set a relaxing tone.

Alternatively, pile on layers of rich, colorful fabric for a spicier setting. A Marrakesh-inspired bedroom might just light the fires of passion! Typically, I advise clients to go for solids or very subtle patterns, since bold designs can be visually stimulating. My favorite exception? Kids' rooms! I love colorful prints there. See "Fast, Fun Touches for Kids' Rooms," on page 132 for more ideas.

- **PILLOWS:** If your pillows are feeling flat, replace them. Be sure to test them out in the store and choose a firmness level that suits the way you sleep. For a full-, queen-, or king-size bed, four pillows are all you need. Accent pillows can create a rich, sumptuous effect if piled high, but don't just throw on one or two. Go all the way or skip them.

A NEW NIGHTSTAND

Furniture stores abound with tables sold specifically for bedside use. But you don't have to limit yourself to these options. A fast, fun way to give your bedroom a fresh look is to revamp your nightstand, or replace it with something entirely new.

- **FORGO THE TABLE ALTOGETHER** and substitute a chair in its place. Pick up an interesting wooden chair at a flea market and paint it. Or recover a chair seat in fabric to coordinate with your bed linens. Add some books, hang a picture (or a few) above, and you have a beautiful vignette.

- **TRY A TOWER OF BOOKS.** This is the fastest way I know to create a nightstand: If you have a great collection of art books, stack some beside the bed in lieu of a table. Top with a small lamp, and you're done. When stacking books, keep in mind that odd numbers tend to look best.

- **REASSIGN ANOTHER PIECE OF FURNITURE.** A petite dresser can do double duty beside a bed, which is a bonus in a small bedroom. You can even limit yourself to a nightstand on just one side of the bed to keep the space open and improve flow.

Supporting Players

Once you have a great bed in place, every other piece of bedroom furniture is secondary. Since space—for dressing, for moving around the bed and making it with ease—is important, fewer furnishings are usually best. This is added incentive to make them pieces you really love.

Look for a side chair that complements the room and feels good, no matter if you're putting on shoes or reading a novel. You'll need a good dresser, in addition to the closet, to accommodate your wardrobe. Having it all in one place makes dressing in the mornings easier and more enjoyable.

And a nightstand or two by the bed is a must (see "A New Nightstand," at left, for imaginative bedside table ideas). That's about it! Kids' rooms, again, are an exception to this rule. See my tips on page 132 on how to outfit them for fun.

Floor Coverings

If you have hardwood floors in your bedroom, great! They look beautiful and are easy to keep clean. But for a cozy bedroom, entirely bare floors are too cold and spare. A quick, cozy update is to buy a sheepskin rug to go next to the bed. Or go for a larger area rug to define the sleeping area.

A side table isn't necessary in the bedroom, but if you have room, go for it. Here, a fun lamp, with multicolored shade made of recycled magazine pages, adds style.

If you have the space, it's nice to carve out a spot for reading, meditating, or just daydreaming in a bedroom. This window nook, outfitted with a Flokati rug and big throw pillows, is a peaceful escape.

SOMETHING NEW UNDERFOOT

Give yourself a full week to shop for a new rug and have it delivered. Some tips:

- **A plush rug,** such as a silk pile rug or a sheepskin, will be really warm and comfy under your bare feet. A small one next to the bed is especially nice when you get up in the morning.

- **A natural fiber,** like sisal or jute, provides warmth and texture, and looks great, too. These aren't as soft underfoot as plusher choices, but they do help dampen noise, which is an added benefit in your sleep space. Their neutral tones make them a good choice to cover a large area; you can layer a softer, smaller rug on top where you need it most.

- **Have wall-to-wall carpet?** Try layering something fun on top, like a wool area rug in a bold color. This is a great, quick way to give the room some personality.

"COMFORT IS PERHAPS THE ULTIMATE LUXURY."

—BILLY BALDWIN

6. Is It a Bath or a Spa?

The bathroom is the center of well-being in a home. In the mornings, it may be the picture of chaos while everyone rushes to get out the door. But in the evenings or on lazy weekend afternoons, it is your own personal oasis to unwind and refresh. And when it's time to entertain, the bathroom provides an opportunity to pamper your guests with chic amenities.

Whether you're inviting friends and family over for a dinner party or preparing for an open house, remember that people will be visiting the bathroom. You want it to be as comfortable and inviting as any other space.

When I visit the home of a client for the first time, I check out the bathroom. Rule number one is that it must be *uber* clean. Not just a quick polish-the-faucet-and-mirror clean, but scrubbed from floor to ceiling, so that you want to be in the space. I tell my clients to think about how good it feels to check into a nice hotel room. Your bathroom should be as clean as one you'd find in the Four Seasons. You should be able to kick off your shoes and walk around barefoot. If you'd rather not go barefoot in your bathroom, it's time to start scrubbing.

Cleaning is a mundane chore, sure, but don't underestimate its power. One of my clients, Stephen, showed me his bathroom and told me he wanted to spruce it up. The basic fixtures were okay, but the room was far from clean. The marble tile was mildewed. The bathtub was gray. He said that the tub came that way, but I wasn't convinced. I told him to pour some bleach into it, fill it up with water, and let it sit overnight. He was ecstatic when he called the next day because when he drained the tub he discovered it was actually sparkling white.

Clean, clear surfaces, a soothing palette— it all adds up to calm. This pristine white bath, sunlit and embellished with a tall bouquet of gladiolus, is a shining example.

To take care of the mildewed tile, he hired a professional cleaner to come in and scrub the walls and floor. Then he dealt with another issue: The shelf above the tub was overflowing with bottles. Each bottle had just a bit of product in it. He chose one shampoo and one shower gel to keep and chucked the rest. That's it. Simple.

A happy bathroom is like a private spa. It radiates calm and harmony. It's sparkling clean, well lit, and decorated with stylish, luxurious accessories. If yours is functional but lacking in warmth—all hard surfaces and harsh task lighting—you're missing out on an opportunity to indulge yourself and your guests.

Don't worry if you don't love every detail of the room. Even if the tiny outdated tub drives you nuts and the drab tile makes you queasy, you can still create your dream bathroom with the speedy tips you'll find in this chapter.

Most decorating challenges in bathrooms take one or more of these forms:

- The room is cluttered and in disrepair (such as leaky faucets and overflowing medicine cabinets).
- The style feels dated or just depressing (tattered towels and an unfashionable color palette).
- The space is functional, but not warm or inviting (lots of cold porcelain and few soft touches).
- The lighting is unflattering.

These issues make a bathroom uncomfortable and unattractive. But they are easy to address. Whether the room you want to update is a master bath (a room that has fantastic potential to be a luxurious suite), a powder room (the tiniest and most "public" of these private spaces), or something in between, the basics are essentially the same.

Little details, like a stack of fluffy towels anchored by a seashell, make for a luxurious room. The grand-scaled armoire provides abundant storage.

A bathroom adorned with unique accessories and artwork feels comfy. Here, botanical prints, a fern in a simple vase, and a vintage map make this room memorable.

As with other rooms in the house, we begin with the foundation. The elements that define every bath—the sink, toilet, shower and tub, vanity—are more or less constant. These are the "bones" of the room, and while you won't likely be able to replace them in a day or a week, you can take steps to make them look their best. Once you've done that, you can focus on the details that really make a difference: texture, lighting, color, and accessories.

In every case, remember that this is speed decorating and you have just a few hours to a week to pull it off. You might feel the urge to call in a contractor and have that bathroom gutted, but now isn't the time for that. We won't be tearing down walls, retiling, or launching into major plumbing projects. Instead, think about doing a thorough detox by cleaning and removing unnecessary stuff. You can update the lighting or a faucet and change accessories and decorative items to create a relaxed vibe.

SIX DETAILS THAT WILL MAKE ANY BATHROOM SHINE

1. **A closed seat:** Make it a habit to keep toilet lids down, always.

2. **Good grout:** Is it stained black with mildew or chipped away in places? Take the time to redo it.

3. **Floors that sparkle:** When you're cleaning, pay attention to corners and hard-to-reach spots, like behind the toilet.

4. **A clear vent:** Vacuum the fan vent routinely so that the bathroom stays moisture-free and the vent remains clear of grimy buildup.

5. **A polished look:** Clean and shine faucets, cabinet hardware, and other metal surfaces so you can see your reflection. Water spots and tarnish make a bathroom dreary.

6. **Candles:** Invest in a scented candle or two to create instant ambience.

Charming vintage details include a brass faucet and apothecary jar on the sink and a large antique mirror that gives the room an expansive feel.

It's easy to give your bathroom a fresh new look without ripping out the tile. New fixtures and decorative details—such as the sconces, fun bud vases, and sheepskin rug in this bath—are fast, high-impact additions.

BATHROOM BASICS

By now, you know how I work. No speed decorating project begins without a thorough evaluation of the situation. Even in such a small room, it pays to take a little time to contemplate before diving into quick fixes.

This step is especially important if your budget is tight or you're overwhelmed with the job. I saw this with JoAnne, a client who wanted to update her bathroom but didn't have the budget for a full-blown renovation. The space was a standard family bathroom—about 5 ft. by 9 ft.—and hopelessly (in her mind) blah. The white tile looked dated, but worse, the grout was dirty and made the whole room appear dingy.

What's more, the lighting was unflattering. There was a glaring fluorescent fixture over the vanity and an unexciting ceiling light.

A pro can help you get your bathroom into spanking-new shape. A fresh coat of white paint and bright lighting enhance this room's soothing atmosphere.

JoAnne was frustrated and wanted to start tearing down tile, but once we sat and talked it through, we found that the real problems were easy to identify. I knew that the advice I gave her (to leave the tile intact, but regrout, a job she could easily do herself, and to replace her light fixtures and accessories) would have dramatic results.

Recruiting the Help You Need

You can do the work on these pages yourself, with a few exceptions. Look at the notes you've taken and think about the work that needs doing.

If your bathroom walls and ceiling are cracked or stained from water damage, you might want to schedule a handyperson to come in and patch. If you see paint bubbling on the ceiling, touch it to see if it's damp. If so, get it checked out by a plumber to make sure there isn't a leak that could surprise you in the future.

The same plumber could install a new faucet or sink. If you want to try wallpaper but aren't confident in your hanging skills, hire someone to come in and do it for you. If you need an electrician to swap out a light fixture or put in a dimmer switch, schedule him now, too.

The trick with hiring a professional is finding someone who is willing to take on small projects. The best place to start is with family and friends—ask around for a referral of someone who has done such jobs in the past. Another option is to ask someone who works at the local hardware or home improvement store. Typically, employees of those stores do small jobs on the side.

●●● DO YOU NEED A PLUMBER?

For the most part, plumbing jobs fall out of the scope of speed decorating. There are times, though, when an old toilet or sink really has to go. Replacing them typically takes a day or so, if you have a talented handyperson or a plumber willing to take on a quick job. Of course, some of you love to get out the toolbox and tackle such projects on a long weekend. If you have the know-how, go for it. Otherwise, don't attempt one of these without picking up the phone.

- **A new toilet:** If you are blessed with a pink toilet, circa 1980, you must rip it out. Replace it with a timeless white toilet, but beware the chain reaction (the floor needs repair, you might as well retile; if you're retiling, the bathtub really should go, too—and suddenly you're in the trenches of a full-blown renovation). A smaller fix-up, like replacing an old plastic toilet seat for a new wood one, can also be a good bet.

- **A new sink:** Bringing in an elegant pedestal sink adds instant style.

- **A new faucet:** This is a quick job for a handyperson (or plumber, if he's already there doing other work) that can make a big difference in the look of a sink and the whole room.

- **A new showerhead:** This can be a great touch of luxury, particularly if you choose one of the rain-style options. Again, a handyperson should be able to take this on.

Clearing surfaces makes room for thoughtfully placed accessories, such as the fresh wildflowers, sea sponge, and chemistry jars filled with bath salts shown here.

Fill bathroom shelves with beautiful items, not clutter. In this bath, stacks of towels, seashells, stones, finely milled soaps, and fresh flowers all combine for a spa-like effect.

The Timeline

You picked up this book because you love instant results. The bathroom is an easy room to transform in a week or less. Painting or regrouting is a quick weekend project. Need a faster makeover? All you need is a few hours to shop for new accessories or to do a deep clean. A week gives you time to indulge in a wider range of shopping options. If you're looking for the perfect medicine cabinet, for example, or a chandelier, you might want to browse antique stores or shop online, which means allowing time for delivery. Likewise, if you need to enlist a handyperson, it's nice to have a few days flexibility in your schedule.

Write down your deadline now. Write it in your calendar and commit to your bathroom makeover. Then take action. You'll be surprised what you can get done.

On the pages that follow, I'll walk you through some common bathroom scenarios and offer speed decorating solutions to transform the look. You'll find something that works for you, whether you have a week or only a few hours.

STARTING FRESH

It's time to free your bathroom from clutter and disrepair. Your bathroom can be a utilitarian space that can easily handle the morning rush and still be stunning.

How do you want to begin your day? Think about how you'd like to feel. I like to meditate in the morning and focus on my goals. When my husband and I moved into our apartment, I knew that would be a challenge because the bathroom had no storage space beyond the medicine cabinet. There was a lot of potential for clutter, which would be stressful rather than soothing.

ULTIMATE
BOOTCAMP

TILE AND TUB REDOS

If your bathroom tile looks dated or dingy, you might think the only solution is tearing it out. But fresh grout will give you a brand new look. This is an easy weekend project. Visit your favorite home improvement store and see what colors of grout are available. Pick up a chip book of grout color samples that you can take home and see what looks best in your bathroom. Make your choice, and then get to work!

Here's another quick fix: If your tub has rust or chipped porcelain, hire a reglazer to come in and spray on a fresh coat. It's like having a new tub. This takes a day or a weekend, depending on how long it takes you to find and schedule someone for the job.

MEDICINE CABINET MAKEOVER

When you go to someone else's house, do you look in their medicine cabinet? Expect that everyone is checking out yours. Here are some tips for getting it in order and looking so good that you'll want your guests to peek.

- **Make sure that the cabinet is clean.** Use glass cleaner on the shelves. Organize products so it's easy to grab what you need.

- **Throw out old or expired bottles.** This is especially important with medicines. As for cosmetics, take a hard look at your products and if there's something you haven't used in a year, toss it. When purchasing new ones, look for beautiful packaging and fragrances that inspire you.

- **As for the cabinet itself, if it is old and painted,** think about stripping off the layers of paint. Many of my clients in New York City have prewar bathrooms with painted-over zinc cabinets; we stripped them down and then had a painter coat the metal with a clear, matte sealer for a clean look.

- **Consider forgoing the cabinet altogether.** If you hate the style of your medicine cabinet, a quick and easy solution is to take it down and replace it with a simple mirror. Then add a freestanding cabinet or side table to catch all those bottles and jars.

A freestanding side table is a stylish alternative to the standard medicine cabinet. This table, in green enameled metal, has a drawer for supplies and shelf space for decorative accessories.

I purchased a simple glass shelf and installed it above the toilet to store fluffy bath towels and just a few of our favorite products. We pared down a lot and got rid of all those extra bottles that we didn't need. We added just a few, well-placed accessories, including a gilded gold baroque mirror that makes the room feel bigger. The basic "bones" of the room are in good shape, and by keeping the rest to a minimum, we've created the perfect space to ease ourselves into the day.

COLOR AND STYLE

After your bathroom is clean and free of clutter, you should be able to step back and really see the room. If what is left makes you want to take it to the next level, this is the time to add stylish accessories and have fun with color.

Many people aren't sure what to do with such little spaces and leave them to the dull bare essentials. It's great to see people get in touch with their inner decorators to make a statement with their bathroom. I had a client who did just that. Her powder room, though clean and functional, felt dated. The paint on the walls, once white, was so old it yellowed. We decided not just to refresh the room, but to inject it with life by painting it a poppy red. The result was a spectacular French bordello feeling.

We added accessories that complemented the walls and removed the drab curtains altogether, replacing them with an adhesive film that had a lace pattern and gave the window the look of acid-etched glass. Natural light filtered into the room but provided privacy. We finished with a large antique mirror to make the room feel bigger.

A bathroom is a great space for bold color, as in this red-tiled room. Paint and coordinating accessories can create a similarly vivid effect. Here, natural accessories, including rose quartz and sea fan and a colorful striped hand towel, give the room distinctive style.

Hanging wallpaper
is fast and can com-
pletely reinvent the
look of a bathroom.
This bath gets a shot
of energetic style
from one wall of
metallic, flocked
paper in a green
floral pattern.

INSTALL NEW HARDWARE

Buy new towel bars and toilet paper holder for a crisp look.
Bed and bath specialty stores have many styles to choose
from, and they come with mounting hardware for easy
installation.

Consider an upgrade for your door hardware, too.
This is a snap to do in a weekend: Go shopping one day,
and install the next!

If you have a bathroom that just feels uninspiring, you can take some quick,
big steps to revive it.

Pick a Color Scheme

Choose something fun, like beach glass green, and go with it. Paint one wall or the
entire bathroom in this spring hue. Another option is to buy all your accessories in
a vibrant color, from shower curtain to trash can, to infuse the room with style. (For
tips on painting and choosing colors, see "A New Paint Job," on page 75.)

Ditch the Curtains

Rather than dealing with fussy, dusty curtains, try an opaque adhesive film (available online or from your home improvement store) applied directly to the window
glass. It comes in a variety of patterns and colors. It's a stylish way to get privacy
and maximize natural light without sacrificing space.

Try Wallpaper

If you're curious about wallpaper but intimidated by the commitment, this is a
great place to try it out. I love metallic papers in bathrooms; they add an element of
offbeat glamour.

Flattering, soothing light is the goal in any bathroom. This bath gets its warmth from a combination of natural light and a well-placed fixture. The light, a frosted-glass, wall-mounted piece, casts a glow that is pleasing, not glaring.

Start with a Theme

Maybe bold color isn't what you're looking for. Perhaps you'd like to inject the room with natural elements for a soothing, spa-like experience (see "Make Your Master Bath a Private Oasis," on page 166 for a detailed look at how this can be done). Or maybe your favorite vacation inspires you. What inspires you about the vacation: Walks on the beach? Sunset? The market? The colorful food? Brainstorm for details you love about the place and recreate the feeling in your bathroom. Whatever style and color theme you choose, use accessories to carry it through the room.

LIGHT THAT FLATTERS

The key to a beautiful bathroom, in addition to keeping it clean and adding distinctive accessories is to have beautiful light. The fixtures you choose should be in a style you like and bright enough for the tasks at hand. They should also cast a light that makes anyone who walks into the room look and feel good.

Banish fluorescent lights. They make your skin look green, wrinkled, and tired. Another great change I made in my own bathroom is that I replaced the fluorescent light above the vanity with an antique light fixture that I love. It was quick, and it makes the room look so much better. It makes me look better, too.

If you're having a dinner party, turn off the overhead light fixture and keep a candle burning for guests. Everyone looks radiant in candlelight. And, as a bonus, if you haven't had time to clean every nook and cranny, those little flaws hide in the shadows.

Fortunately, less-than-perfect bathroom lighting is easy to fix—fast!

GIVE YOUR POWDER ROOM A MAKEOVER

The powder room is maybe the smallest room in your house and one of the most visited by guests. When you're entertaining, small details make a difference.

Once I received a call from my client Nancy who was throwing a party and needed help, fast. She felt her powder room was really sterile and unwelcoming, and it was. The ceiling fixture was missing and there were some wires hanging in its place. There was one hand towel and a bar of soap. And there was no art on the drab white walls.

I gave her a shopping list of accessories—new guest towels (white monogrammed towels with hemstitch), a grapefruit scented Diptyque candle, and a silver mint julep cup filled with white parrot tulips. We also found a little stool made of nickel and bamboo with a white leather top, which was the perfect spot for guests to set down a purse or sit and freshen up lipstick. An elegant new ceiling fixture on a dimmer—a black Baccarat crystal chandelier—finished the room and gave it a look that really reflected her style.

If, like Nancy, you feel your powder room needs a boost, it's time to send yourself to Boot Camp. You can give this space a dramatic makeover in a few days to a week. Start by thinking about the room through the eyes of your guests: What will make them comfortable? Make a list of the things you'd want if you were a guest in a friend's home.

Here are some tips to get you started:

- **Consider color.** Plain white can be blah. Repainting or adding wallpaper is one solution, but you can also add colorful accessories and artwork to brighten the space.

- **Lighten up.** The lighting should be flattering. When you look in the mirror, you should feel good about yourself. If you don't, shop for a new fixture and put it on a dimmer. (See "Light That Flatters" on the facing page for more ideas.)

- **Have a seat.** If space allows, a powder room should have a place to sit and freshen makeup, or, at the very least, to set down a purse. Indulge your guests with a comfy stool or pretty side table.

- **Add a scent.** Is the fragrance in the room pleasant? A smattering of naturally scented candles creates a lovely aroma.

- **Keep up with the tiny details.** Hand towels should be crisp and clean, flowers should be fresh and standing tall. Keep a stash of special soaps just for company. These are signs of a thoughtful host.

MAKE YOUR MASTER BATH A PRIVATE OASIS

A master bath can be a place to create your ultimate personal home spa. I've seen master baths that were spacious but cold and impersonal, with too many hard porcelain surfaces and too few soft elements; I've also seen bathrooms that, from a decorative viewpoint, just didn't suit the couple that was using it each day.

One couple I worked with, Amy and Rob, had just moved into a beautiful Victorian home with lots of original wood-work and molding details. The master bath had a pedestal sink and claw-foot tub, but, thanks to the previous owner, the walls were painted pink. Rob told me that whenever he went in there he felt uncomfortable because the space was just too feminine. To address that, we chose a classic and, more important, gender-neutral stormy blue to paint the walls and added soft gray accessories. The effect was instantly more balanced.

There are many ways to soften a bath to give it a sensuous, harmonious vibe. The most important thing to do is add texture. Texture is all about touch. My favorite way to add texture is by layering organic natural accessories. This balances both feminine and masculine energy, and walking into a bathroom decorated this way, you feel transported to a spa.

Here are some ways to get this look:

- **If the walls are a boring color,** repaint in a shade that reminds you of your favorite vacation, such as beach sand or cerulean blue or sea foam green.

- **Look for cabinet hardware** and even a new doorknob in materials inspired by nature. A doorknob might be leather on the exterior and glass inside. For cabinet hardware, you might choose brass pieces shaped like tree branches or leaves to give the feeling of bringing the outdoors inside.

- **Add simple white orchids** planted with moss in a clear glass cylinder.

- **Buy accessories made of natural materials** such as sea sponges, organic cotton towels and shower curtain, limestone soap dish, and a wood bathmat.

- **If the space is especially tight,** install a mirror to increase the light and make the room feel bigger. This enhances the natural light, reflecting sunlight into an area that would otherwise be dark. And a long wall mirror can increase the sense of space in a narrow bathroom.

- **Finish with some indulgent touches:** Install a rain-style showerhead. Buy organic products in attractive bottles and lather yourself in creamy lotions, delicious hair products, and bath salts. Buy a beautiful mirrored tray to display them. Have plush slippers and a robe clean and ready to use.

This unique, three-armed sconce is a stylish choice for a mirror side light.

Install Sconces

If the lights above or around the vanity are harsh (if they are fluorescent or sconces with exposed bulbs), swap them out. Install sconces on both sides of the mirror. Sconces that cast light upward are much softer and more flattering.

Try a Chandelier

A bathroom, even a tiny powder room, is a fun place to install a chandelier. Choose one that suits the scale of the room, and be sure to measure so that there's plenty of clearance for the door to open and close freely. Have it wired in place of an existing ceiling fixture or simply hang it from a hook and swag the cord to a corner and run it down the wall to the nearest outlet. The look is instant glamour.

Use a Dimmer

Have a dimmer switch installed so you can adjust the brightness as required. This is smart for every style of light. You can turn up the light for makeup application or shaving, then bring it down for a bath or dinner guests.

Go for the Unexpected

If ceiling fixtures cast a harsh light, replace them. Look for an unusual light fixture or hardware at antique stores or online to really express your personality. (See "Light That Flatters," on page 164, for more ideas.)

Don't Forget Candles

Light a few and you have a cozy setting for a bath. Beeswax candles burn nicely and have a pleasant aroma. Just be careful because too many fragrances can give you a headache. If you're lighting a big room, pick white unscented votive candles to provide light, and add just one scented candle. Lavender is a relaxing choice.

"A MORNING-GLORY AT MY WINDOW SATISFIES ME
MORE THAN THE METAPHYSICS OF BOOKS."

—WALT WHITMAN

7. Beyond Curb Appeal

The yard is your first and best opportunity to show the world you care. And that glimpse of beauty is a generous gift for passersby, too.

Around sunset at our house, my husband and I like to take a walk to see what's going on with the yard. We look at what is blooming, what has died, and what needs improvement to keep the yard looking its best.

We also like to walk along the road and see what others see when they drive past the house. It's a fun ritual, and our efforts reflect for everyone to see.

Outside, creating an inviting home means striking a balance with nature and making sure everything looks good. Your guests will notice these things when they arrive for a party. And if you're selling your home, that amazing first impression may mean the difference between a potential buyer who is excited to see the property and one who drives away without making an offer. It's critical to spruce up the outdoors before having the first open house.

Speed decorating outdoors, just as anywhere else, means making quick fixes. In this chapter we aren't going to be changing the basic landscape of your yard, training romantic vines along a trellis, or putting in that swimming pool you've always wanted. We'll tackle only projects to complete in a week or less. And don't worry—there are plenty of them.

Outdoor living is a beautiful thing. Here, a picnic table, with a collection of teak chairs and benches arranged around it, is set for a magical garden party. Candelabras, cut flowers, and a magenta tablecloth create a festive scene.

Placing some healthy, blooming plants, such as these potted red geraniums and yellow marigolds, near the front door is a quick way to add color.

You can't hurry Mother Nature, but you can make sure she's putting her best face forward. What I'm talking about is a well-groomed lawn, properly trimmed hedges, and some thoughtfully placed plantings. These basic details show the world a home where the owners care. We'll also make sure your house façade is well kept and attractive. And I'll give you ideas for some fast, stylish additions that will make your outdoors truly great.

The most common outdoor decorating challenges I see are:

- A neglected, messy appearance (forgotten bikes and toys, an overgrown lawn and shrubs that make the landscape hard to navigate, and an uncared for façade and windows).

- Poorly lighted property (outdoor lighting is barely there, so the front door, walkway, sidewalk, and yard are in shadows).

- A forgotten outdoor room (patio, porch, or deck aren't as comfy or stylish as they could be).

Great news for the speed decorator: A lot of what is wrong outside your home is fixable fast. If you're hosting a weekend barbecue and need things to look good, pronto, the tips in this chapter are for you. This is a strategy for instant curb appeal. I'll show you how to get the place spiffed up, how to highlight a tree or other asset on the property, and more.

THE FIRST LOOK

Indoors or out, the way I work is the same. The process begins with an evaluation of the situation. Fed up with the mess outside your door? Fantastic! This will motivate you to work toward fast results. To begin, take a step back and try to see the place as if you're seeing it for the very first time. Go through the "Speed Decorating Questionnaire," on page 19. Then set your timeline before taking action.

While you're assessing the situation, take digital photos of your house and yard from all angles. Looking over the photos will help you pinpoint areas that need improvement. It will also help you see the property as others see it.

Rustic stone steps leading up to a pair of French doors make for a charming entry at the home of my friends Kemper and Paul. Flowering herbs grow in pots by the door, and a set of oars leaning against the outside wall hint at the fun activities that await visitors.

Creating a home for a Buddha statue among newly planted birch trees and butterfly bushes is a speedy way to make a personal statement and to carve out a peaceful meditation space in your yard.

Evaluate your yard for possible additions. With the help of a few chairs, a bench, and a stump for an impromptu coffee table, this quiet corner transforms into an outdoor living room.

Evaluating and prioritizing is never as important as when you are in a rush. My friends Kemper and Paul live near us on Shelter Island. They have a ranch-style house surrounded by a bamboo forest and a huge yard, in which they created many outdoor rooms. They love to kick off the summer season with their annual Memorial Day pool party. Both have intense professional jobs, so they rarely have more than a couple days to prepare.

Their evaluation begins with basic cleanup: raking the yard and removing all debris. Then they look around the yard to find plants that died over the winter. They remove the stragglers, and then head to the local nursery to stock up on annuals that are already in bloom. This is a bit of an investment but well worth it; it gives the front yard and sides of the house a boost of instant color.

Similarly, they give their front door a welcoming appeal by framing it with pots of cascading flowers. They fill the pool area with potted blooming hibiscus, strawberries, and palm trees. Overall, it feels like St. Tropez even though it's only the first weekend of the summer. Because they always start with a careful plan, this impressive work can be done in practically no time.

Take a cue from Kemper and Paul when evaluating your own space, no matter your time frame, and begin with a critical look around. Make sure your landscaping is attractive (not riddled with weeds or dead plants or overgrown shrubs) and that items like toys and sports equipment are out of sight.

Check that the lighting is cheerful and welcoming, particularly around pathways and at entrances. And look carefully at the house itself, too. Maybe you've stopped seeing those dingy windows and that peeling paint, but you can be sure your guests will notice. Finally, if you have an outdoor room, be it a quiet sunset-

MAGIC-WAND MAKEOVER — FIVE STEPS TO INSTANT CURB APPEAL

If you only have a little time, do these five things. Work quickly, and you can finish it all in a day.

1. **GET RID OF THE JUNK.** Put bikes away, store trash cans in a garage or shed, clean up scattered toys, toss dead plants.

2. **CUT THE GRASS.**

3. **MAKE SURE THE SHRUBS** have appropriate haircuts.

4. **WASH THE WINDOWS.**

5. **REMOVE STRAGGLY PLANTS** from window boxes and put in fresh flowers.

If you like to cook outdoors, think about setting up a designated grilling spot away from the action. My friends Mimi and Steve created this graveled area for the grill, well removed from where the kids run around and play.

watching spot on the patio or a full-fledged "living room," make sure it's comfortable, well furnished, and attractive.

Once you've evaluated your outdoor space, you'll want to set a deadline for getting the work done. A deadline will really light a motivational fire to get you started. So if you don't already have an official on-sale date for your house or a party in the calendar, make one up. Invite friends over for a barbecue, write the date in your calendar, and get moving.

The tasks you prioritized in the evaluation questionnaire will dictate how you work. I find it incredibly satisfying to work on outdoor projects because so much can be accomplished so quickly.

Of course, if you don't feel like putting in a ton of manual labor, you can hire some help to get the work done. Call a landscaping service to trim the hedges or recruit a neighborhood kid to paint the fence. You might need a few extra days to schedule the help, but do it if your time frame and budget allows.

If you have a full week, you can indulge in some bigger changes. Shop around for just the right outdoor furniture, or plant a few trees to enhance your yard. Whatever the time frame, I have solutions for you.

Thoughtful landscaping sets off your yard's best assets. Here, a lush lawn and shrubbery give this gorgeously accessorized swimming pool the look of a tropical paradise.

Your front door can be friendly and super-stylish, too. This red door with glass panes is fresh and bold and provides a happy dash of color to greet guests.

A FRIENDLY ENTRANCE

The front door is the key to a welcoming home. It should be cheerily lit. The house number should be easy to spot. The door itself (and porch if you have one) and walkway leading up to it should be in good repair. If the paint is peeling or just looks dingy, make repainting a priority. And naturally, if there are any broken spindles on the porch railing, damaged steps, or other details in need of fixing get to those right away.

Of course, the front door should be more than just "in good shape." It is a great chance to make a statement, as my friends Sue and Frank have done with their welcoming entrance. Their home is a beautiful old Victorian with a spacious front porch. The door is original to the house, and the light fixture is a bright, charming antique. Hanging flower baskets abound. They've set up a table with chairs so they can sit with their guests and have appetizers on summer evenings. I always feel excited and welcome when I go to their house.

Welcoming Style

There are many ways to make a style statement at your front door. One of the easiest is by adding a bright new coat of paint. A door in a bold hue, like red, is vibrant and cheerful and can refresh the look of your home—even from a distance. This is a terrific speed decorating task; the door can be repainted in a day, and what a difference! It's an instant facelift.

Planters and furniture around the door and on the porch offer other fast decorating opportunities. You don't need a lot here, but a well-placed hanging plant or a low, lush planter along the walk approaching the door can really energize your entrance.

MINI BOOT CAMP

HAVE FUN WITH HOUSE NUMBERS

These are what people use to find you, so post them prominently. They should also offer a little clue into your style. Replacing them is an easy project done in a couple days, including time for shopping around to find your favorite look. Check the resource section of the hardware store, or search online for funky pop art–inspired numbers and other uncommon options. (Design Within Reach at DWR.com, and design stores like it, is a good place to look for modern ones.)

If you have a covered porch and enough space, consider adding a bench, swing, or rocking chair, and perhaps a small dining set, too. It's the perfect place to watch the neighborhood, talk with friends, or sit in the morning with a cup of coffee. I love waking up early in the summer and sitting on my porch with a frothy cappuccino and my journal before everyone is awake. Another great addition if you have the space? A hammock. There's nothing better than a nap on the porch on a lazy afternoon.

And don't forget the doormat! This says welcome—literally—and goes a long way toward protecting your floors inside the house, too.

Of course, other doors matter, too. Many of us forgo the front door most of the time and enter through the side or back, so make sure those entries also shine. You may not have a house number posted at these entrances, but they still represent your home and greet your visitors. They should be well lit and in the best possible shape.

●●● PLANTERS AT ANY TIME OF YEAR

Whether they're lining your front porch or back patio, planters are a convenient way to add life outdoors. Dramatically faster than planting a border garden or hedge, these little self-contained "gardens" are a speed decorator's friend. Even tiny window boxes can make a big statement. So don't let them die out when the weather turns cool!

Here are some ideas for filling those planters for big impact, no matter the season:

- **WINTER:** For instant festive glow, wrap mini fir trees in tiny white lights.

- **SPRING:** Plant tulips or hyacinth.

- **SUMMER:** Try geraniums and cascading ivy for a French feeling. Outside the kitchen door or window, plant herbs. They grow quickly and are as useful as they are beautiful.

- **FALL:** Arrange gourds and dried leaves.

A Bright Welcome

Good lighting is another essential. At the door, an inviting light lets guests know you're home and ready for visitors. You can quickly enhance your house's curb appeal by upgrading this light. Begin with replacing the fixture if it's old or in bad condition or if it doesn't suit the style of your house.

Consider the scale and level of formality of the entrance when making your choice. In my old farmhouse, for instance, we kept the original schoolhouse fixture. The base is a little rusty but I think it adds character. (It doesn't have to be brand new to look good.) Shop around at flea markets and antique stores or online for a fixture that matches the style of your home. At the very least, clean away the cobwebs from your existing fixture, and replace a weak bulb so it shines brightly.

Think about lighting the pathway that leads up to the door, as well. If you don't already have them, consider installing lights along the driveway and walk,

Planters with evergreen shrubs, like these holly trees, look great at the door and are low maintenance.

A wide front porch can be a comfortable extension of your living space. Here, a cozy throw tossed over a swing and lush potted plants and hanging baskets give the front porch a lively yet homey atmosphere.

179

Big windows make a
mirror-like backdrop
to an inviting patio
and lush backyard.
Remember, the big-
ger those panes of
glass are, the more
vital it is to keep
them clean.

so visitors will have no trouble finding their way. Spotlights and uplights made specifically for outdoor use can be a speed decorator's best friend. You can use them not only to illuminate your house but also to highlight landscape features.

You can add any number of bright features to your yard in as little as a few hours, though I recommend allowing a weekend so you can shop one day and install the next. A great, sparkling clean front door or porch light is a start, but don't stop there. You can add any of these bright features to your yard in as little as a few hours, though I recommend allowing a weekend so you can shop one day and install the next.

- Wrap strands of white lights around your favorite tree. This doesn't have to be a holiday-season thing. Tiny white lights are appropriate all year and add a pleasant, festive glow.

- Place uplights made for outdoor use (available at home improvement stores) to illuminate the front of the house. You can also use them at the base of a tree, aimed upward through the branches, to set it off and create an enchanting warm welcome. Use heavy-duty, outdoor extension cords and a timer, so they'll turn on as the light falls in the evening.

- To shed light on a pathway, try solar lights. These come in many styles and are easy and fast to set up.

ON THE OUTSIDE, LOOKING IN

Once you've gotten the entrance into shape, it's time to turn your attention to the façade of the house itself. In particular, look at the windows. Chances are, if you make sure your windows sparkle, the entire house will glow.

Clean windows may seem obvious but often are overlooked. Recently, when I was helping a homeowner prepare her place to sell, she complained about the lack of light inside. The windows were so dingy it looked like they hadn't been washed in years, and the screens were filthy. Once we had them cleaned, the rooms felt fresh and new.

WASH THOSE WINDOWS!

Washing windows is a tough job, no doubt about it, but one that pays big dividends in your home's appearance. You can do it yourself in a day, or hire someone else to get to work. You'll love your newfound sparkle. Here are some tips to get done fast:

- **WASH WITH A SOLUTION** of distilled white vinegar and water. This works quickly and well and is the perfect green alternative to chemical-based products.

- **WIPE WITH NEWSPRINT** to help prevent streaks. I also like microfiber cloths, because they are lint-free and work well with water alone.

- **HIRE A PROFESSIONAL** window service to wash the windows. They have special equipment to get the hard to reach ones, particularly on the upper levels. A professional can get the job done safely and quickly.

- **ASK THE SERVICE** if they pressure-wash window screens—a chore most of us don't want to contemplate, so let someone else do it!

So the first, fastest, and most basic thing you can do is wash the windows. Do every one, inside and out. Hire someone if the task is too onerous. You'll want to look at the shutters, too, if you have them. If the paint is peeling, or if you think the color is blah, have them repainted. Alternatively, consider removing them altogether if they aren't functional.

Window boxes are a great way to make a statement. Some people think of them as decorating opportunities only in the spring and summer, and they let them go dead in the cooler months. But I say they can and should be beautiful all year. And since they're small planters, getting them in good shape is an easy task even when you're in a hurry. (See "Planters at Any Time of Year," on page 178 for inspiration.)

GORGEOUS GREENERY

Congratulations. Your front door and house are ready to show off. Now it's time to look around at your property. If you're lucky enough to have a lawn and garden, you need to make sure they're looking their best.

Careful tending of greenery can really make your yard look beautiful. I saw this the first time I visited my friend Gary's home. His yard had an enchanted feeling. He had a vegetable garden, an herb garden, shaded garden of hostas and ferns, and a number of outdoor rooms. Winding among them was a simple mowed path. It was so inspiring that I had to include it in this book!

Landscape Basics

Landscaping can be a full-time job. Think topiaries, trimmed privet hedges, and complicated flower border gardens. These can be wonderful details, but for the speed decorator they are entirely too fussy. For a beautiful yard, you only have to master the basics. If you'd prefer to leave the work to the professionals, then simply hire someone and keep a schedule to make sure it gets done, flawlessly.

It's simple: If your grass is too long, pull out that mower and cut it. If your shrubs look shaggy, trim them. Don't forget to clean up the details, like the grass bordering walkways and around the mailbox.

Windows are the eyes of a home. Keep them in top condition. Here, a sparkling clean window with freshly painted, white trim makes a house look crisp and new.

Fast-growing grasses like these are a delight for the speed decorator. Okay, they won't grow in a weekend, but they fill in an empty space with breathtaking speed: Plant in June and they'll be cascading by July.

A variegated border of plants, stones, and potted tropical trees surrounds a swimming pool.

While you're outside, examine the condition of the walkways and patio stones. If any stones are cracked or damaged, repair or replace them to avoid a potential disaster like tripping and falling. You can do this quickly yourself; in fact, I recently put a slate path in our yard. It was hard work but done in a couple days. I just borrowed a flat shovel from a neighbor, dug out the grass, placed each stone, and then repositioned the patches of grass. Visit a stone supplier for the pieces you need.

Border Gardens and Other Delights

To add color and beauty to a bare exterior, try flowers. There are few solutions speedier than running to the local nursery and buying whatever blooms are in season to brighten up the porch or the borders along the sides of the house. I suggest buying local, indigenous plants. Have fun and experiment for a look you like. This is pricey, but worth it. By creating beautiful borders, you'll be adding to the value of your home.

If this is too expensive, pick one area to work on and let the rest be for now. You don't have to do everything. We're on nearly two acres and are taking it a little at a time. This year I worked on removing the old deer-eaten shrubs from the front and

Backyard luxury: A pair of striped lounge chairs arranged under a blooming tree in my friend Gary's garden. A nearby bar is set up with fixings for tropical drinks.

Want a superfast outdoor dining room? Set a table and chairs on the patio. Add some accessories, like these big flowering branches in an oversized vase, and you're party-ready.

planting local holly trees in their place. I saved on mulch by having the local dump bring a truckload. It's important to pick an area and work within your budget.

During the growing seasons, you might also look for herbs and edible flowers that are ready for transplanting. You can put together an herb garden for instant beauty and have fresh flavor right outside your door for cooking. I really love edible flowers. Nasturtiums are vibrant orange and red and look great around the house. They also lend a delicious, peppery bite to salads.

OUTDOOR ROOMS

When decorating outdoors, think of the space as an extension of your home where you can create different "rooms." Be creative and have fun setting them up.

The most basic outdoor rooms are the patio or deck, but these days, more and more people are really living outside. When I visit my clients' homes, I see outdoor kitchens and dining areas, outdoor living rooms, even outdoor bedrooms! Forget about adding square footage to your house; if you want more living space, at least in the warmer months, expanding outdoors is the thing to do.

You might go Zen and create a meditation area, or group Adirondack chairs in an ideal sunset-watching spot. Or go all out and set up an outdoor dining room fit for a party. Your guests will be thrilled. You can use furniture to define distinct spaces. The deck can become an outdoor living room. The porch can be the place to play games or have dinner parties. You could even build a tree house for kids and adults.

And, of course, if you're planning to sell your home, an outdoor room is a bonus. Make the space really livable and inviting, and those buyers will feel like they're getting a lot more for their money.

One of my friends loves to entertain outside, and he made the perfect spot for it. He installed a Dutch-style door at the back of his house and outside of it laid a blue stone patio. He bought four comfy teak chairs and arranged them around a fire pit. Altogether, the setting was ideal for an outdoor summer evening.

A quick way to borrow this look is to buy four chairs with comfortable cushions and arrange them on a patio. Outfit your room with a copper fire pit, which is fast to buy and set up. If you have a room like this, take the time to get it into shape. If you don't, there are plenty of speedy ways to add one. Look around and consider the potential of your space; play up the best features of the property with some great furnishings and accessories.

GET "INSTANT" PRIVACY

Feeling a little too cozy with the neighbors? An attractive fence can be a good solution. But if that seems too extreme, you can get similar privacy with well-placed plantings. Visit your local nursery for advice on trees that thrive in your area and that are available in a decent size. You can easily buy them, have them delivered, and plant them in a week's time. Just be sure to consult with the nursery on planting techniques and timing.

When we bought our farmhouse, the backyard was overgrown with neglected trees and vines. We had everything cleared, but that left us with zero privacy. Our solution was to stagger locally indigenous trees such as white pine, holly, and juniper around the perimeter. They allow for flow yet shield us from the neighbors. This is a pricey solution but a beautiful one. You can make the cost more manageable by adding just a few at a time; we're still adding at our house.

If privacy isn't your top concern, try a row of smaller shrubs. That can add a bit of interest to an otherwise undistinguished yard or a stark length of fence. Either way, this quick project can make a huge difference in the look of your home.

PLAY UP YOUR PORCH

Want to add an outdoor room? You may be overlooking one you already have. A porch is often a missed opportunity, a place where you come and go but never really linger. Outfit it with a few key furnishings, and it will become a comfortable, practical room in its own right. There's no construction necessary here, so you can easily create this new room in a week's time. Some details to consider:

- **Begin by measuring your porch.** You may have a sense of how much furniture you can accommodate here, but taking measurements with you to the store will help in choosing specific pieces.

- **Look for furniture that will hold up to the elements.** Even though a porch is covered, it is still subject to wind and wet. Pieces made for outdoor use will have durable fabrics and rustproof metals. Rugged antiques, in wood or wrought iron, can work well, too.

- **Add a rug.** This can help define a seating or dining area, particularly on a large porch. Look for one made for indoor/outdoor use.

- **Think about double-duty pieces.** An ottoman can also be a side table or an extra seat; a loveseat or bench is great for lounging and for pulling up to the table for dining.

- **Consider foldaway pieces for a small or narrow porch.** A drop-leaf table and folding chairs can be set up for an outdoor meal and then cleared for easy access afterward.

- **Add accessories to pull everything together.** Decorative accents are important, even when the view is the primary attraction. Plants, vases of flowers, table linens, pillows, and cushions will give the space the unified look of a real room. Those cushy pieces will also make outdoor furniture a whole lot more comfortable.

Arrange your furniture with the view in mind. Here, a grouping of Adirondack chairs around a fire pit overlooks a creek—perfect for sunset watching.

If you want to entertain outdoors, consider features that allow for easy access. Here, a Dutch-style door is perfect for backyard dining and serving.

A teak coffee table, rugged enough to live outside, serves as an impromptu sideboard for serving.

Outdoor Furniture

The kinds of pieces you'll need outdoors will depend on the kind of room you want. A few chairs and tables are essentials. For a charming conversation space, you might want to add a bench and coffee table. For cooking and dining, include a sideboard and food-prep area as well as a dining table. If you'd like to cozy up outdoors for a snooze, add a chaise lounge or a hammock.

When choosing furniture, look for weatherproof pieces. I like teak for outdoors because it requires little maintenance and develops a beautiful silvery gray color as it weathers. Weatherproof upholstery is available in many styles; we bought director's chairs in white weatherproof fabric and they fold up easily in the winter for storage.

As for your existing outdoor furniture, now's the time to give it a facelift. Throw slipcovers in the wash, or if they're in bad shape, buy new ones. Replace them all at once, so everything looks crisp. If you have rusting metal furniture, you can buy products to clean it. Just take care to follow the manufacturer's advice. For rusty stainless steel, try using fine steel wool and olive oil to bring the luster back.

Tropical blooms and brightly colored dishes set the scene for a festive pool party.

A swimming pool surrounded by nature requires little decoration or fuss. Here, some potted plants and a pair of lounge chairs do the job.

A patio is an ideal spot for an outdoor room, since it's so easy to place furniture. The stone path here is similar to the one I put in my own yard and is an easy do-it-yourself project.

The Yard and Beyond

Take advantage of the view, wherever it happens to be best. Set up some chairs and ottomans in the yard so you can watch the sunset. There's no rule that says you have to stay on the porch.

A quiet corner of the yard can also be perfect for a chat or cup of tea. Arrange a nice bench, a couple of chairs, and a coffee table for an ad-hoc, yet inviting, living room area.

If you have a pool, make the most of it! There's no better spot for a party on a summer afternoon. You can use accessories to give the pool area great style. Stick with a color theme such as orange and white or blue and white for a nautical theme. It's easy to go bold with color around a pool. Create an area for relaxing with chaise lounges, benches, and side tables. And don't forget a big basket of brightly colored towels for guests.

Colorful place settings and numerous candles make for a perfect summer evening dinner party.

A full outdoor kitchen is a great luxury, if not a fast addition. The speed decorator can easily mimic such a scene: Set up all-weather furniture, like teak, near the grill, and add accessories in shades of green to complement the setting. In a long weekend, you can even lay down stones to steady the table and give the dining area an air of permanence.

Candles complete the dining table. Here, a selection of white pillars in glass hurricanes rings a gazebo, providing an enchanted glow.

Light Up the Night

Torches are great to keep bugs away. And since there's no power source required, they couldn't be faster to set up. You can use them to anchor your outdoor room by lining them up behind a table or group of chairs.

And don't forget candles. Place pillars in tall glass hurricanes or jars to protect them from the wind, and use them to line a dining table or porch rail. I was so excited to find a stash of old Mason jars in the cellar of our farmhouse. I use these in the summer filled with sand and votives for the perfect magical evening.

Though this elegant model entices the little ones, a tree house isn't just for kids anymore. What grown-up would refuse a nap in that hammock?

It takes time to grow an impressive stand of trees, but bamboo is a fast (and inexpensive) privacy solution. It grows remarkably quick. Be sure to do some research about controlling its spread before planting or your neighbors might not be too pleased.

Resources: PLACES I LOVE

ACCESSORIES

Associated Cut Flower Co., Inc.
131 West 28th Street
New York, NY 10001
212-695-6100
associatedcutflowers.com

**Berdgorf Goodman
Decorative Home on Seven**
754 Fifth Avenue
New York, NY 10019
800-558-1855
bergdorfgoodman.com

CB2
800-606-6252
cb2.com

Celadon
21 North Ferry Rd.
Shelter Island, NY 11964
631-749-5429

Chiasso
877-CHIASSO
chiasso.com

Decorati
415-227-4558
decorati.com

Design Boom
designboom.com

Design Public
800-506-6541
designpublic.com

Environment 337
337 Smith Street
Brooklyn, NY 11231
718-522-1767
e337.com

MoMA Store
800-851-4509
momastore.org

Moss
866-902-3423
mossonline.com

The Paris Apartment
theparisapartment.com
917-749-5089

Plow & Hearth
800-494-7544
plowhearth.com

Sur La Table
800-243-0852
surlatable.com

Target
800-591-3869
target.com

Thé à la Menthe
13 Grand Avenue
Shelter Island, NY 11965
917-887-2401
courtenayo@mac.com

West Elm
888-922-4119
westelm.com

Z Galleries
443 Broadway
New York, NY 10013
800-908-6748
zgallerie.com

ART

Boltax Gallery
21 North Ferry Road
Shelter Island, NY 11964
631-749-4062
boltaxgallery.com

Condé Naste Archive
Sarah Walker-Martin
condenaststore.com
212-630-2714
thenewyorkerstore.com

Julie Maren
303.641.6764
juliemaren.com

Rod Massey
grovelandgallery.com
612-822-9120

BATHROOM

Bed Bath & Beyond
800-462-3966
bedbathandbeyond.com

Designer Plumbing
866-232-8238
designerplumbing.com

eFaucets
800-891-0896
efaucets.com

Quality Bath
800-554-3210
qualitybath.com

Sonoma Forge
800-330-5553
sonomaforge.com

Waterworks
60 Backus Avenue
Danbury, CT 06810
800-899-6757
waterworks.com

DECORATIVE HARDWARE
Drawer pulls, cabinet knobs, hinges, doorknobs, towel bars

The Brass Center
248 East 58th Street
New York, NY 10022
212-421-0090
thebrasscenter.com

Digs
888-868-DIGS
digs.com

My Knobs
245 Old Country Road
Carle Place, NY 11514
866-MyKnobs
myknobs.com

Restoration Hardware
800-910-9836
restorationhardware.com

Simon's Hardware
421 Third Avenue
New York, NY 10016
888-2-SIMONS
simonshardware.com

Wainlands
24–60 47th Street
Astoria, NY 11103
800-843-9237
wainlands.com

COUNTERTOPS & CABINETS

Formica
800-FORMICA
formica.com

R G New York Tile, Inc.
225 West 29th Street
New York, NY 10001
212-629-0712

DONATE

Dress for Success
212-532-1922
dressforsuccess.org

Housing Works
143 West 17th Street
New York, NY 10011
212-366-0820
housingworks.org

Salvation Army
800-SA-TRUCK
salvationarmyusa.org

FLOORS

ABC Carpet & Home
888 Broadway
New York, NY 10003
212-473-3000
abchome.com

Anthropologie
800-309-2500
anthropologie.com

Crate & Barrel
800-967-6696
crateandbarrel.com

Flor
866-281-3567
flor.com

Odegard Rugs
212-545-0069
odegardinc.com

FURNITURE

3 Square Design
888-333-8440
3squaredesign.com

Aero
Thomas O'Brian
419 Broome Street
New York, NY 10013
212-966-1500
aerostudios.com

Ballard Designs
800-536-7551
ballarddesigns.com

The Barbara Barry Collection at Baker
800-592-2537
kohlerinteriors.com

Blu Dot
612-782-1844
bludot.com

Curran Online
800-555-6653
curranonline.com

Desiron
151 Wooster Street
New York, NY 10012
212-353-2600
desiron.com

Dune
88 Franklin Street
New York, NY 10013
212-925-6171
dune-ny.com

Horchow
877-944-9888
horchow.com

Ikea
800-434-IKEA
ikea.com

Jonathan Adler
47 Greene Street
New York, NY 10013
212-941-8950
jonathanadler.com

Just Scandinavian
161 Hudson Street
212-334-2556
justscandinavian.com

Knoll
76 Ninth Avenue, 11th Floor
New York, NY 10011
877-615-6655
knoll.com

McGuire Furniture
mcguirefurniture.com

Neiman Marcus
888-888-4757
neimanmarcus.com

Room and Board
105 Wooster Street
New York, NY 10012
212-334-4343
roomandboard.com

Safavieh Home Furnishings
902 Broadway
New York, NY 10010
212-477-1234
safaviehhome.com

SUITE New York
625 Madison Ave, Suite 218
New York, NY 10022
212-421-3300
suiteny.com

Williams-Sonoma Home
888-922-4108
wshome.com

KIDS

DucDuc
524 Broadway, Suite 206
New York, NY 10012
212-226-1868
ducducnyc.com

Harmoine Interieure
harmonie-interieure.com

Land of Nod
800-933-9904
landofnod.com

Pacifier
310 E. Hennepin Ave.
Minneapolis, MN 55414
888-623-8123
pacifieronline.com

LIGHTING

LIGHTS I LOVE:
Glo-Ball, Jasper Morrison
Random Suspension Light, Moooi
Archimoon, Philippe Starck
Arco Floor Light, Flos

RESOURCES CONTINUED

Black Gold Candelabra,
Ineke Hans
Baccarat Zenith Chandelier
Spun Floor Lamp,
Sebastian Wrong for Flos
KNAPPA Lamp, Ikea Brylle/
Jacobsen
Samtid Floor Lamp, Ikea
Collage Pendant, Louis Poulsen
PH Artichoke, Louis Poulsen

Boyd Lighting
415-778-4300
boydlighting.com

Hive
820 NW Glisan
Portland, OR 97209
866-663-4483
hivemodern.com

Lighting by Gregory
158 Bowery Street
New York, NY 10012
800-807-1826
lightingbygregory.com

Lighting on the Net
877-5MY-BULB
lightingonthenet.com

Ochre Furniture
212-414-4332
ochre.net

LINENS

Bellino Fine Linens
18 West Forest Avenue
Englewood, NJ 07631
201-568-5255
bellinofinelinens.com

Boomerang for Modern
2475 Kettner Street
San Diego, CA 92101
619-239-2040
boomerangformodern.com

Garnet Hill
800-870-3513
garnethill.com

Gracious Home
1220 Third Avenue
New York, NY 10021
800-338-7809
gracioushome.com

Hastens
80 Greene Street
New York, NY 10013
212-219-8022
hastens.com

Marimekko
1262 Third Avenue
New York, NY 10021
800-527-0624
marimekko.fi/eng

Matteo
888-MATTEO-1
matteohome.com

Schweitzer Linen
1132 Madison Avenue
New York, NY 10028
212-249-8361
schweitzerlinen.com

Viva Terra
800-233-6011
vivaterra.com

ORGANIZING SOLUTIONS
Coat racks, closet systems, shelves, baskets, umbrella stands, bookcases, shelving

Atlas East
718-596-5045
atlaseast.com

Container Store
888-CONTAIN
containerstore.com

Gotham Organizers
Lisa Zaslow
212-866-9493
gothamorganizers.com

Iss Designs
949-366-0780
issdesigns.com

Kartell US, Inc.
39 Greene Street
New York, NY 10013
212-966-6665
kartellus.com

Luminaire
800-645-7250
luminaire.com

Milder Office, Inc.
97 N.10th Street, 201
Brooklyn, NY 11211
718-387-0767
milderoffice.com

OUTDOOR

Cheap Sam's
631-654-3020
cheapsamsplantbargains.com

Conran Shop
407 East 59th Street
New York, NY 10022
866-755-9079
conranusa.com

Deck Tiles
212-695-5334
decktiles.org

Lowe's
800-445-6937
lowes.com

TABLETOP

Barney's
888-222-7639
barneys.com

Global Table
107–109 Sullivan Street
New York, NY 10012
212-431-5839
globaltable.com

Heath Factory
400 Gate Five Road
Sausalito, CA 94965
415-332-3732 x13
heathceramics.com

Hermès
691 Madison Avenue
New York, NY 10065
212-751-3181
usa.hermes.com

Kim Seybert
55 A-2 Main Street
East Hampton, NY 11937
631-329-6200
kimseybert.com

Loaves & Fishes Cookshop
2422 Montauk Highway
Bridgehampton, NY 11932
631-537-6066
landfcookshop.com

Rosenthal China
201-804-8000
rosenthalchina.com

Pearl River
477 Broadway
New York, NY 10013
212-431-4770
pearlriver.com

Rose and Radish
460 Gough Street
San Francisco, CA 94102
415-864-4988
roseandradish.com

Sarah Cihat
sarahcihat.com

What Would Mikey Drink?
whatwouldmikeydrink.com

RECYCLED FURNITURE & VINTAGE ACCESSORIES

1st Dibs
1stdibs.com

The Demolition Depot
212-860-1138
demolitiondepot.com

eBay
ebay.com

Home 114
21 North Ferry Road
Shelter Island, NY 11964
631-749-1811
home114collection.com

Olde Good Things
124 West 24th Street
New York, NY 10011
888-551-7333
oldegoodthings.com

Marika's
6 South Ferry Road
Shelter Island, NY 11964
631-749-1168
marikasantiques.com

Scrapile
scrapile.com

WALLS

Benjamin Moore Paints
benjaminmoore.com

Blik
866-262-BLIK
whatisblik.com

decoradar | murals + spaces
917-981-8804
decoradar.com

Flavor Paper
504-944-0447
flavorleague.com

Mibo
813-832-5263
mibo.co.uk

Pratt & Lambert
800-BUY-PRATT
prattandlambert.com

INDEX